# HUSTLE
### AND
# GAME

Craig A. Massey

Copyright © 2018 Craig A. Massey
All rights reserved
First Edition

NEWMAN SPRINGS PUBLISHING
320 Broad Street
Red Bank, NJ 07701

First originally published by Newman Springs Publishing 2018

ISBN 978-1-64096-444-0 (Paperback)
ISBN 978-1-64096-445-7 (Digital)

Printed in the United States of America

To you, the reader.

We are only limited to the rules and regulations
of the world in which we choose to live.
—Joanna Kay Lakin

# Chapter 1

# Game Is

Life games reflect life aims.

THIS BOOK TEACHES DIFFERENT STRATEGIES and technics that can be used to gain the hearts and minds of others through the art of game, as people have become absentminded as to what things they can do to attract the things they want out of life. Much like this book you hold in your hand now, it's only because you feel it has something to offer you that has you drawn to it as you will have to have something to offer others yourself in the efforts to draw others to you as well.

It is through the three parts of game, physical, mental, and verbal, accompanied with the right strategies and technics that this is possible. The word *game* refers to the word *knowledge*. This knowledge is power and is key in stepping your game up. When you have game, you will have the ability to read people and know exactly what it is they want. Of course, this is only so that you can use it against them so that you can get what you want as this is the goal in running game—to get what it is that you want.

Another part of running game is being able to sell yourself. You must be able to create an image that is desired by an unsuspecting party all in an effort to gain whatever it is this other person has that you desire so much. Through the years, these strategies and technics have become watered down as they have been passed down from generation to generation. The result is we are left with all these people that have figured out a way to use people, although they lack any real knowledge of game or what game is about.

Having game is having the ability to draw people to you so that you can gain their hearts and minds. Once you have gained the hearts and minds of others, you will have the power of persuasion over these people. The power of persuasion is key to your success as it is this persuasion that will allow you to dominate these people so they may be used to your liking. Another key to being successful at running game is to make sure your intentions are in the right place as there are many people that have been able to gain the power of persuasion over people, but their intentions are poor and of the self-loathing nature.

Having game can be looked at as a business, business of self, and we are in the business of selling dreams.

To do so, you will be required to sell yourself verbally, just as any business owner does.

They sell the ideas and possibilities that their business brings to the table. To do so, they must sell themselves. They must gain the trust of others, and to do so, they must appear trustworthy.

As first impressions are typically very important, it is within these first impressions that a person decides if a person is trustworthy or not. So image is everything, and you must be sure to protect your image at all costs.

The object of the game is to gain the hearts and minds of others so that you will have a better chance of succeeding it. It is when you have the hearts and minds of the people around you, working to help you succeed and achieve your goals, that you will find yourself to be successful. The game is played to win as all games what you gain out of playing the game will be based on your level of expectations. The game is about advancement. You advance by playing on other people's weaknesses, desires, and needs, all in an effort to gain from them in some type of way to do, so you must have something they desire.

This is because if you have nothing to offer, then nobody will see a reason to invest themselves and their time into you as this person will see spending time and energy on you as a waste of resources and time.

You may always have something to offer by investing in yourself, making yourself the thing that is valued the most overall.

So it is very important to keep up your appearance and to be able to provide the types of qualities that will make you desirable.

The fact of the matter is that people are all too selfish to the point that it affects them in a negative way. The only real way that we can improve ourselves is to start from within ourselves. It is through improving in ourselves and who we are as people that we will be able to improve our lives. As people, we have become okay with the level we have reached within ourselves, and so we are okay with who we are as people, forgetting the endless possibilities that await us.

We fail to continue to better our lives as we have become so caught up in the lives that we have already built for ourselves. It is only when our lives have become unmanageable that we see a problem with the things that we are doing with ourselves.

We should be welcoming hurdles that life throws at us as we should be turning them into stepping-stones that are used to advance us in life as we stay forever bettering our lives. It is my opinion that if you want to have game, then you should work on yourself in the sense of who you are as a person. This is so that others will be attracted to you in a positive way for your own self-betterment, as you can be sure many people may be attracted to you now but for their own selfish reasons.

These people should be the hurdles that shall be turned into the stepping-stones used to advance you in your life. These are the hurdles that most people sidestep, if possible, and when not, they end up eating the brunt of it financially or mentally. As a person could spend a lifetime beat down by the hurdles that we face with, most of these hurdles having first and last names, we cannot exchange our self-dignity, our religious beliefs, our money, or freedom in an exchange for a watered-down friend or lover. We cannot consume our lives with trying to hold down those that have wronged us.

We must start being good to ourselves and stop hating others for doing wrong unto us when we wrong ourselves daily. It is my opinion that we should stop trying for what others have by taking it as it is much easier if we just allow them to give it to us instead.

As they may have a new incentive provided by you, it is provided through new perspective. As you will learn in this book, it is through new perspective that you will bring about new thoughts and new possibilities. These new possibilities bring about newly found hope that a person will hang on to as they feel they have found it within you.

## Gaming In

Gaming someone in works like this: you want to provide a new perspective on things. This is so the person you are looking to game in will suddenly see things in a new light with new hopes and new thoughts that bring about new possibilities for a person. There are two key elements that plague us as people, and they are money and loyalty. These are two issues you will always be able to play off of as money and loyalty are underlying issues. These underlying issues provide people with the things they need in life, and they are typically the things people tend to lack as well. It is important to know what a person lacks because it will tell you what they want or desire, as it will always be the thing that a person does not have that they will desire, and it is through providing what one desires that will draw them to you.

Although all you really need to know about a person is there direction, it is the direction that a person is heading in will be a good giveaway as to what they need and desire. There are many other things that people need besides the obvious things like feelings of importance, as everyone wants to feel important, and they desire it so much that they will be willing to do anything to get it as everyone wants to belong and to feel as if they're somebody important. These are just a few different things that will draw people to you. However, when it comes to direction, one's direction or goal for themselves can be seen within where they spend their time.

As another word for direction can be the word *goal*, when you know a person's goal for in which they intend to achieve. Then you will know their needs as the things they need will be seen within what is needed to achieve this goal. The idea is to use this knowledge of their needs against them so you can make a feel as if you know their needs better than they do. This is so that you can make them feel as if you yourself are capable of fulfilling these needs. This will give you an advantage over others, as most people are only worried about their own needs.

However, you must remember that you're providing solutions to other people's problems in an effort to gain what it is you want. These solutions are ideal-type solutions that incorporate yourself into them.

Much like the businessman that provides possible solutions, you want to point yourself out to be part of the solution. Like when we're talking about money, you don't want to provide money, but the idea is that you provide a solution for money. And when we're talking about loyalty, you don't necessarily need to provide it for someone but by making them think that you are. You will be able to provide a solution that will work to draw them in.

When a person hears the word *loyalty*, there are typically a range of different ideas on what that word may mean. Typically, people think this means someone that won't cheat on you. Well, loyalty can also simply mean someone that won't do you wrong or screw you over whether it's in a friendship, partnership, or any other type of relationship. So loyalty can be presented in many different ways. There again, the idea is to make or present yourself somewhere within the solution. The power of humor is also a very powerful tool used to draw people in so that you may gain the opportunity to gain the heart and mind.

Humor or laughter is typically a replacement for both loyalty and money, as people will trade both money and loyalty for a little bit of happiness. This happiness usually comes with a good laugh, and it is through a good laugh that you may bring happiness to someone.

## Humor

Laughter brings happiness, and the ability to make people happy and happiness is what it's all about. It's the driving force behind everything, as all people have the desire to be happy. Every penny earned and every penny spent is done with the idea that it will provide happiness. This is exactly what you should be looking to do for someone when running game. You look to provide happiness. Much like a business provides relief and happiness for someone, you do too. By making people happy, you can gain a place in the hearts and minds of these people. As everybody will always find time for a good laugh, you will find that people will always find time for you if and when you can make them laugh.

Laughter is very important, and as my grandma would say, it's good for the soul. In a book I recently read written by Allen Klien called *The Healing Power of Laughter*, it talks about how humor has the power to take us away for a moment, even if just for a moment. It is within that moment that a person can feel a sense of relief from all stress they may be feeling. Something that really caught my attention while reading this book is how laughter not only brings people together but it also provides new perspective for someone.

Having a healthy sense of humor is what makes a person funny. A healthy sense of humor can come from being able to poke fun at a situation at hand. To do so, you will be required to see things from the other side as there will usually be a funny sort of ironic twist to most things in life. It is being able to see this other side that can bring about new perspective for someone. So humor or laughter is an awesome way to incorporate into your game as it works so well because it is an unsuspecting strategy, and it works to draw people to you without them ever suspecting it. Just as anytime someone attempts to speak to you, it can be seen as them reaching out to you.

This is why laughter works so well because it can be seen from a distance without ever having to reach out to anyone. As anytime you reach out to someone, it can be seen as being needy, as anytime someone reaches out to a person, they typically need something.

It is through laughter you may reach out to someone in a manner that is unseen. It is my opinion: the best way to reach out to someone is not necessarily using words but by letting your personality shine through. By being funny, you can let your personality do the talking for you.

# HUSTLE AND GAME

## Three Parts of Game

There are three parts to game, and they are physical, mental, and verbal. The most important and most effective is physical. Being up on your physical game is to say that you are keeping up your appearance. A good example of someone that is keeping up their appearance is women, not all but most women are up on their physical game as some of the most beautiful women get up in the morning looking terrible. However, it doesn't matter what obstacles they may face physically. They find a way to address these issues whether it be a wig they wear or tons of makeup, lipstick, etc. By the time they are finished getting dressed, these women are looking good. They look so good. There are typically many, many men looking for a chance to get close to these women. This is because they are up on their physical game, and this is why you are so attracted to them because they are attractive.

So if you want people to be attracted to you, then you will need to be attractive. It must seem obvious that if these women were to get up in the morning and were to do the minimal as far as getting dressed for the day, you can imagine the different response that one would get if they went through their day looking like a hot mess. It would be a very different response than the one they will get when they are looking attractive. This is why you must keep up your physical appearance as your appearance is also what determines your image. And your image is very important to running game as your image will determine how others look at you.

It is typically the deciding factor in how they treat you as well. This doesn't mean that you won't have people attracted to you if you are unattractive.

It simply means they will be attracted to you for another reason. However, you want people to be attracted to you for reasons that will benefit you, not for reasons that will take from you in who you are as a person. It has been my experience that people want to be with the most attractive person possible, leaving behind people that may be funny or attractive in another way that's not physical. Your physical game is the most important and typically the deciding factor when it comes to whether a person is interested in you or not.

Your mental game is going to be the next important thing you can add to your game. As your mental game is all about your thought process, one of the most important things your mental game brings to the table is protection from others as you must have a strong mindset to be able to play the games that others will throw at you. And you must keep your mind strong so that you can make sure you're ahead of the game, and the only way to do this is to stay up on your mental game. This means you must know who you are and what you bring to the table as well as know what will attract others to you. When you have a good mental game, you will be able to play good mental games as well, as there are many games you can play in an effort to get people to do what you want them to. For example, say a person has a lot of money, and you want them to give you some. You could say something like "You never give me any money" in an effort to get them to want to prove you wrong. They may just give you some money. Similar to this game, we have the backward game. The backward game works like this: you basically tell a person everything they're doing but in a backward manner.

By backward manner, I mean, you take whoever they really are and what they really do and tell them the exact opposite. This strategy will work if your goal is to get up under someone's skin as people hate to be accused of doing something they're not doing.

Now you might say, "Why would I want to get up under somebody's skin and intentionally make them mad?"

Well, there are a number of reasons. Typically, people will do this in an effort to start a fight as they may be looking for an excuse to leave or maybe they are looking to take you for a ride on that emotional roller coaster. That emotional roller coaster is full of emotions, and it is through emotions that feelings are brought about as it is typically the goal of anyone running game—to create feelings inside of someone. There are many, many other games that will be described throughout this book. However, these are just a few examples given to show how important it is to stay up on your mental game.

Finally, we have verbal. Verbal is the least important when it comes to running game. However, it is a part of having game as you will be required to speak to people if you want to spark up any type of relationship, as many people have issues with being able to talk.

This has brought about a large number of people that have become concerned with their verbal game. It is my opinion that if one was to keep up on the first two parts of game that one can do just fine without ever needing to be worried about the last part, which is the verbal, although you must be able to draw people to yourself in one manner or another. When you are up on all three parts of game, you may consider yourself to be game tight. You will need to speak to people in the terms they understand. Unfortunately, people only pay attention to the things they're interested in. Now a person may gain interest in you through your verbal game, but you must find a way to talk about things they're interested in. As we talked about, if you're not sure what they are interested in, money and loyalty always draw people in. If you can't come up with anything to say, I suggest you don't worry about it. Verbal game is really about just having the guts to speak to someone as the truth is. It doesn't matter what you say to a person unless you plan on telling some lies to draw them in, as any person is attracted to you for the things you say. This could be a negative reason behind them doing so, and by that, I mean negative for yourself as this person may have an ulterior motive for being around you.

Another thing your verbal game is good for is to be able to present these thoughts and ideas to someone. So if you want to be up on your verbal game, I suggest you work on the first two parts of game. Again, those parts are physical and mental. This is because for you to have good verbal game, you will need to have a good mental game. Keeping up on your physical game will make your approach and the end result of the situation much better than ever expected. These are your three parts of game: your physical, mental, and verbal. If you're looking to step your game up, then you should be working on these three every day. In everything that you do throughout your day, you should practice these three.

## Thoughts

Everything starts with thoughts. Thoughts bring about emotions, and emotions are what creates feelings. Creating feelings is very important as it is within these feelings that you will gain the hearts of others. To do so, we must first start with the mind. You want to create little nagging thoughts that will cause a person to go on an emotional roller coaster. This roller coaster is brought about by the unknown as it is the unknown that causes a person to think.

It is these thoughts that we create that we will be playing off of, as in any situation whenever faced with a dilemma where one is forced to weigh out the possibilities.

You will find that there will typically be three different outcomes that a person will have in their head. There will be the best possible outcome, the worst possible outcome, and the most likely outcome. It is the not knowing that tends to drive people crazy and puts them on this roller coaster of emotions. We do so by creating a range of different possibilities for someone to throw around in their head. Bill Cosby once said, "All you have to do is get their attention. Once you do, you can tell them what you want." This is true as people are going to believe what they want to believe anyway.

So the real goal is to draw them in. Once you do that, you're already in the door as your first goal is to just get a person to start thinking about you. As we have been discussing, there are many ways to do that.

With your overall goal being to gain the heart and mind, you must know that by the time you gain the heart you have already gained the mind. However, it is through these thoughts of unknown possibilities that you will create the emotions necessary to bring about feelings.

Thoughts.
Emotions.
Feelings.
Action.

It is common for people to become caught up in the moment. Then they feel they have found the thing they've been looking for.

This is why it is important that you are not looking for someone to fulfill your needs as you may become lost in the moment when you feel you have found that person that has your needs met. When you become lost in the moment, it is typically because someone has created the ideal person that you are looking for. This person may seem ideal as any imperfections that may seem apparent will typically be overlooked or excused as these things only get in the way of the ideal situation that one may be hoping for.

When people get lost in the moment, they tend to follow their emotions wherever they may take them, forgetting any bad thoughts and dismissing any thoughts that will prevent them from feelings of bliss, allowing themselves to live in the moment. It is my opinion that you should not allow yourself to get caught up in the moment that others created for you. This is because this moment is typically filled with wild emotions along with the feeling that may allow you to feel good at the moment. However, when the moment is gone, so are the feelings, and you will now be left with nothing.

It is your job to create the moment that others will get caught up in. This moment is created when you create the ideal situation for someone. You can do this by making yourself the ideal person that one would love to meet. You can become this person by having whatever it is you feel they may be lacking in their life. We do this so that a person may live out their fantasy with you for the moment as only in their fantasies and wildest dreams would they meet a person like you. In this moment, a person will feel as if everything has aligned and all is possible as they live in the moment you created by making yourself the person they needed in their time of need.

This moment can be created by simply turning up the charm. Like a nob on a stereo, you can simply turn up the charm, as it can be seen in a person that desires to draw someone in. They can easily put a smile on their face, acting as if everything a person says is interesting or funny then really it's not. This is done in an effort to draw someone in and to allow a person to live in the moment. This is exactly why. Although we look to create the moment for others to live in, we avoid living in the moment ourselves because we know it is created through superficial actions in an effort to win someone over.

# Chapter 2

# Build 'Em Up, Tear 'Em Down

> As long as you keep a person down, one part of you
> has to be down there to hold them down, so it means
> you cannot soar as you otherwise would.
> —Marion Anderson

THIS CHAPTER IS DEDICATED TO building people up and tearing them down. As many people will look to do both, it is very important for you to know how these strategies are done and how they work as there are many strategies that are used to do both. First, we'll start with breaking people down. As I mentioned, there are many ways to do so. One of the ways to do so is by taking face. You can take face by proving someone wrong, as nobody wants to be proven wrong. Proving someone wrong hurts them more than you know.

If you can't prove someone wrong in a logical way, you can always prove them wrong in an emotional way. This would mean instead of pointing out something they have done physically, you can always point out something they have done emotionally.

This would mean instead of pointing out any one event or action that you may feel they have wronged you, you would point out how you feel about something. Then you would point them out to be the person that makes you feel that way, all in an effort to make someone feel as they are wrong or have wronged you.

When you make a person feel as if they are wrong or as if they have wronged you, it makes them feel bad or ashamed of the things they have done. The worse they feel, the more beaten down they become. This is a well-known strategy for someone that wishes to beat a person down by taking face of a person and proving them to be wrong in the things they're doing and how they are doing them. You will be able to recognize this strategy easily because it must be obvious to one that you are aware of what you do. Therefore you know what you don't do when someone accuses you of doing something that you know you're not doing.

It must be because someone is attempting to use this strategy on you. This strategy works so well because it causes a person to feel as if they need to do something to make right with you or the thing they have done wrong to you.

When people are looking to tear you down, they will look to push you outside of your comfort zone, outside your boundaries in which you feel secured in your ability to control the situation at hand.

In a book I recently read called *The Temper of Our Time* written by Eric Hoffer. He says when you push someone outside their boundaries, they will also lose their identity. As drastic change creates an estrangement from one's self, it generates a need for a new birth. This means you can strip a person from their identity by pushing them outside their comfort zone, causing them to view themselves in a new way. As everyone must have an identity, a person will start to recreate themselves based upon their newly established, new perspective of self.

This strategy is used by people when they are looking to get you to conform to their liking. As their way of life or living may be very different than the one you are used to, so they use this strategy to break you down and strip you of your nature. Simply by dragging you out of your comfort zone, it must be an early warning sign. Anytime someone looks to drag you out into the open, they are doing so because they have ulterior motives for doing so.

By dragging a person out into the open, I mean mentally of course, there are many ways a person will look to do so by keeping things very casual. Not putting any effort or feelings on the table, they will also tell you the things you want to hear, tiptoeing around any actual, real explanation of how they feel. They won't call you for days to check and see how you are but then suddenly act as if they care. These are all ways of dragging you out into the open to where you are left with your feelings out on the table for everyone to see.

These are all strategies meant to drag your feelings and emotions out into the open as these strategies work to drag your feelings out to the surface and leave you in the open. Another strategy people will try is through words, as words are very powerful. They have the power to make a person feel good or bad about themselves. It is through words that the ego and pride are built up or torn down. The ego is based upon how a person feels that other people view them, and the pride is based upon how a person views themselves.

The ego and pride are the things that people will look to break down in an effort to break you down.

So if you are looking to break someone down yourself, you may look to break down the ego and pride as well.

First, we'll start with the ego. The ego is based on how a person feels that other people see or look at one's self as a person can become pumped up with feelings of greatness or great shame. Depending on how a person feels that other people are viewing them, the ego is what feeds the pride that a person holds on to when thinking of one's self. We start with ego because the ego is also the easiest to break down.

The ego is broken down by proving to a person that others are viewing them in a negative way. This is done by pointing out the negative things that they are doing. Then you point out the obvious which is how others view these activities accompanied with your thoughts and how you are feeling about them, as this is a typical strategy of people that wish to harm you. Then they can't harm you directly. They will start in the areas that they can which is usually at a distance through your friends and people you know.

Even if these ideas that you are feeding to a person aren't true as long as the one's ego in which you intend to break down are affected in a negative way, then you can be sure you are on the way to breaking down their walls of pride, ego, and the walls of entrapment in which cases a person from being harmed as it is through strongholds of the mind that need to be broken down.

That this ego and pride will become broken, then these strongholds are breached. A stronghold of the mind is something that is embedded deep in a person's mind. It is a strong belief that has become embedded so deep within a person to where they no longer have control over their own thoughts. This is what causes a person to no longer have control over their actions as well.

Pride is broken down only after the ego has become broken down as the pride is based upon how a person feels about themselves. As when a person's pride is broken, it's because they no longer feel the pressure of upholding the persona they once had. A person's pride can be broken when you make someone feel differently about themselves through new perspective, making them see things in a new light as pride can be broken down by proving someone wrong in the things they do, the things they say, and the things they believe in to where a person no longer prides themselves in being who they are as the person they are has become inadequate.

In a book written by Joyce Meyers called *Battlefield of the Mind*, he talks about how thoughts control our actions. These thoughts are brought about by words. These words are sometimes what control our actions. These words don't have to be spoken once they become imbedded in a person's head. In her book *Battlefield of the Mind*, he says these words can bombard our minds with lies and cleaver-devised patterns of nagging thoughts that bring about depression, oppression, and doubt. That is accompanied with fear that causes our minds to wonder and stretch as we try to find rational reasonings and theories to ease our minds. This is exactly how people are broken down. They're playing on their insecurities, their weaknesses and fears and the things that really bother them the most. It is the reasoning and theory that gets to people, followed by their unknowing of truth. Any type of loss will typically break people down as well. The word *loss* ensues that something has been taken from them as it is easy to take physical gains.

However, it is much harder to take mental gains from people. So it is very easy to break a person down physically, especially when they value physical items.

It is through the heart and mind that a person is broken down mentally as it is through the heart and mind that a person's pride and ego may be broken down as well. It is through strongholds of the mind that a person keeps their ego, pride, and mind-sets of authority. To break a stronghold of the mind, we must work on these in a counterproductive way for the other person. The objective is to play on a person's fears and feelings of inadequacy, all in an effort to break a person down. Just as positive strongholds are created through hearing positive things, they will also be broken in. This way, however, instead of hearing the positive, it is through hearing the negative things that a positive stronghold of the mind is broken. Once a person hears the words that you wish to implant in their mind, it is their own theory and reasoning that will be used to carry out the rest. This is a great strategy used to tear people down because you're actually using someone's mind against themselves. By creating a negative stronghold within a person, you can use someone's mind against themselves, allowing the person to tear themselves down.

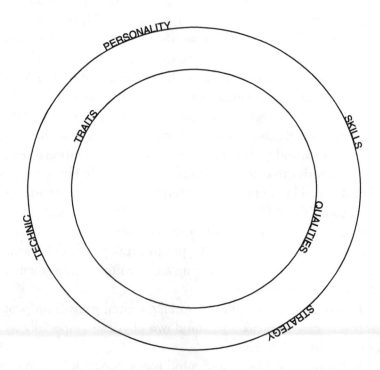

In the picture, it shows a circle with the word *stronghold* written in the middle. This will represent a strong or deep belief that a person believes in. The words *pride* and *ego* are written on the outside of the circle. This is because you will have to break through the pride and ego to ever be able to break a stronghold. On the outside of the circle are the words *personality*, and this is because the personality will have to be broken through first as the personality can be faked and is typically used to protect someone. Either way, if you are looking to break someone down or build them up, you will go through the same order of process.

When it comes to building people up, there is only one reason you would ever want to build a person up, and that is because they build you up. So before you ever decide to build a person up, I ask the question: "Do they build you up as a person and in who you are?" By this, I mean, do they use their time being involved in actively building you up? Of course, this means both physically and mentally. This is a very important question for you to ask yourself because you want people in your life that you can build up.

You need people in your life that you can build up. This is because in order for a person to be able to build you up, they need to be in the position to do so. If someone is not building you up, then they're tearing you down. Do you want to avoid these types of people? Of course, if you want someone in your life that builds you up, you must be willing to offer the same. A good rule of thumb is if a person makes your life better, then I would say you need that person in your life, but if they make your life worse, then you don't need them in your life. If this is the case, then you definitely don't want to be looking to build them up in any kind of way.

You build a person up just as you would tear them down by boosting their ego which lifts their pride, and when you raise a person's pride, their personality will start to show more as this person becomes more comfortable with who they are. This is brought about through raising their ego so they pride themselves in who they are. This causes a person to show one's true self which allows a person to feel okay with who they are.

This is also a great strategy for drawing people in, as people are drawn to people that makes one feel as if they can be themselves.

Building people up consists of many things, as you can build a person up mentally or physically.

It is my opinion that it is more important and more effective to build a person up mentally. Although people love the physical things that life has to offer, it is the mental things that are much harder to come by. Building a person up mentally makes a person feel good and is an important part of boosting the ego and pride that they have.

Physical things can be gained anywhere; however, mental gains cannot be. A person's status among the community, status among peers and family members all have an effect on a person's pride and ego as these things usually determine how a person feels. They are viewed by the public which has an effect on how they feel about themselves. When you build a person up mentally, be aware that their newly-found self may view things differently, including how they view the very same person that built them their ego and their pride up as a result. People become complacent and forget just who they really are deep down inside.

To build someone up or tear them down, you'll need to get their attention first. You can do so by touching on key elements and beliefs that a person already has instilled within themselves already. If you're not sure what these things may be, an easy way to find out is by allowing the other person to inadvertently tell you about themselves. As people love to talk about themselves, they will tell you who they think they are and how they think they are. These characteristics and traits are typically not true and tend to be how they would like to be or how they would like to seem to others. It is typical for these people to point out all their bad traits as actually being good traits.

They will excuse off any bad traits as good traits, explaining them off as actions of circumstance or maybe just a reaction to someone else's actions, as they feel justified in doing so. This makes them feel as if they're coming off as fair or innocent when really what they are doing is letting you know things about themselves that they think you want to hear. They have now talked themselves into trying to win you over as this person now suddenly seems to care about what you think of them.

As they try to convince you they are who they say they are, they now care about what you think and value your opinion. It's time to build up their sense of who they are. You do so by confirming what we already know they want to hear. These will be the things they already told us about themselves. It is now important to make yourself seem as if you are a peer, as if you are the same exact way that they are. This way you allow the other person a moment to agree with you and the things you are saying.

It is important for you to act equally as happy as you want them to be by meeting you. This will bring up their spirits and optimism, making the other person feel equally as happy and equally as important as you want them to make you feel. So although you are aware of your actions and what result they will bring, the other person is left to get lost in the moment you created for them. One of the things people desire the most is to belong. It gives people purpose and a reason to live.

It makes people feel alive, or for you to make a person feel as if they belong, you yourself must belong. This doesn't mean you must belong to any group, cult, or gang. This means you must belong to yourself as you are unique. You are your own person. You love yourself and not just saying you love yourself but by actually loving yourself. This means you respect yourself in every way. You do not allow others to disrespect you in any way. And you show to yourself and others just how much you love yourself by taking really good care of yourself.

People are drawn to people that take good care of themselves because it shows that you'll take good care of them, if given the opportunity. These strategies are designed to build people up either physically, mentally, or just for the moment.

You must be aware that building people up can be dangerous to you and your success, so you want to be sure the people you are looking to build up have the same intentions for you in mind except for when it comes to building people up just for the moment so they can be lost in the moment you created.

If you feel like a person may be built up too much to the point they feel they can't be touched, you may have to knock them off of their high horse. To do this, you may have to do something drastic, something they never expected. This is a necessary strategy when someone starts to disrespect you and treat you as a lesser than. When someone is on their high horse, they will feel untouchable in their position up on their high horse. Taking someone off their high horse is done by attacking their ego and pride. This is because it is their ego and pride that they are riding on.

To do something drastic that comes as a surprise to someone, you will look to the one thing they never expected. It might be another male or female to unexpectedly answer your cell phone or a sudden change of heart. It could be just telling a person the word *no*. The list goes on and on, whatever it is you want to attack the ego and pride. This is because when you attack the ego and pride of someone, it causes emotional insecurities that bring about worry, anger, and stress, and it is the worry and stress they will be left to ride on.

# Chapter 3

# Playing Games

> If I am not for myself, who is for me? And if I am only
> for myself, what am I? And if not now, then when?
>
> —Hillel

WHEN PLAYING GAMES WITH PEOPLE, you want to make sure you are not beaten at your own game. You can do so by making rules for your game. These rules are meant to keep you in the winning position at all times. As you begin to construct a mental map of the game in your head, you may picture it as a structure, and inside this structure is where this game is played. Although your structure may take any shape you wish, this structure represents the mind. Now as the saying goes, life games reflect life aims. This means the end result of your game should reflect your overall goal in which you intend to reach. Your game must be set up to enroll new players constantly.

This is because without players, there is no game. Now one of the number one things people playing games of any type fail to see is that the game cannot become cynical. It cannot become some sick way of harming people. All in the effort to get the things you want out of people, as in any game, it must be a game worth playing. It is my opinion the game should be played by giving people what they want. Although your overall goal is to get what you want in an effort to get people to want to play this game, it will need to start out providing them with what they want.

Now how you act will determine how you are looked at by the players. This means you must hold yourself up to the highest possible standards. There is typically a strategy to all games. I suggest you set in play a strategic set of moves. These moves should trump all, and depending on what your overall game goal is, these moves should either leave a person stumped or basically confused to the point they feel they are somewhere between figuring out the game or giving up. You must keep in mind to make plays that will not be played back on to yourself. Basically, do not put yourself in a position to where you allow anyone to confuse you in an effort to stay ahead of the game and the rest of the players. A good rule of thumb I strongly suggest is to stay two moves ahead. As most people aren't that thrifty to be able to guess your next move, they surely won't be able to guess your next two moves for sure. This means you know your next two moves and your opponent's next two moves as well. You want to make sure that your game is better than the other games out there.

You want your game to have purpose and meaning in which members can be measured and valued. One of the most important things to remember is that you must form a sense of relationship with the other players, as this is what makes them feel a sense of equality. This is important because, without it, nobody will ever be willing to play your game.

In a book written by Michael E. Gerber called *The E Myth Revisited*, he talks about playing games in a work-type setting. Coming from an employer's point of view, he talks about ways to be successful through playing games with the employees. He lists a set of rules devised to be basic rules of engagement for the game. Here are the set of rules he gives. Keep in mind I have altered rules 1, 3, 5, and 6 along with eliminating rule 8.

Rule No. 1: Figure out what you want your people to do then make a game out of it by making a game out of utilizing the strengths other people bring, all in an effort to get what you want out of the relationship. This is effective because it seems relationships are carried on as long as the people in them are getting the things they desire out of them. Although people will tell you they don't like playing games with themselves and others, I assure you, people are drawn to playing games of every sort. It is when a person starts to think of the things they are doing as a game that they will typically start to feel themselves, as they will be drawn to a game when they feel as if they are playing one.

Rule No. 2: Never create a game for your people that you are unwilling to play yourself.

If you yourself are unwilling to go through the harsh realities of the game you created, what makes you think that anyone else will be willing to either? You must take into consideration what the player is getting out of playing this game. Although you will want them to put in more than they are getting out of playing this game, it is up to you to make sure they feel as if they are gaining in some way or another. You don't want another player to feel as if they are clearly putting in way more than they are getting out of it.

Rule No. 3: Do not play against yourself.

By this, I mean, don't play yourself. There are many ways you can begin to start playing yourself without even knowing it. This is very important as it is the person that creates rules to keep them safe, such as the seven rules listed. That ends up playing themselves when they don't follow the very rules they created, as everybody has needs and the desire to fulfill those needs as well. If you aren't fulfilling those needs, they will get fulfilled elsewhere. Another way that people play themselves is by assuming that because another person doesn't speak about something doesn't mean they don't know about it, and nobody is stupid, so I suggest that you don't treat them like they are. This is because I feel it would be harmful to the success of running game.

Rule No. 4: Change the game from time to time, the tactics not the strategy.

You want to change the game at times because it keeps things fun, as a person that doesn't change up the game from time to time plays a stale game. You want to stay ever changing and forever advancing, building and changing up the game. It also keeps people from guessing your next move which is very important because you need to stay ahead of your own game. Your tactics are going to be your approach or method that you use when you are running games on people. You don't want to change your strategy because your strategy is going to be your plan of action. So you may change your tactics, but you want to end up still working toward the same goal you intend to reach.

Rule No. 5: Expect the game to be self-sustaining. People need reminder of it all the time.

This game isn't going anywhere as everybody likes to play games. So anybody that doesn't want to play may be made aware that there will always be someone to take their place. However, this rule, like all rules, are set up by us, so this rule is also for us. All it really is, is as a reminder to ourselves that the game we play will sustain itself when played right.

Rule No. 6: The game needs to make sense or cause confusion.

You want your game to always make sense to one's self, and although it may make sense to others at times, the number one goal to this game is to cause confusion. This will have people stumped or dumbfounded which will have them stuck even more and drawn into trying to figure the game you are playing out.

Rule No. 7: The game needs to be fun from time to time.

This is because if your game is not fun, nobody will want to play it. Although the game can't be fun for everyone all the time, it must be fun from time to time to keep the game self-sustaining.

These rules are a basic set of rules that you can start your game off of. Although you may add to them, you may also change them so that they may fit the game you wish to play. However, I strongly suggest you base your game off of these rules as they have already been set up to run a sustaining and successful game.

I have included some of these games people will play in the effort to get you to do what they want.

These games are listed in the back of the book. These are the keys to game. They will be the key in your success in running game. They are understanding, direction, communication, intention, and providing new perspective.

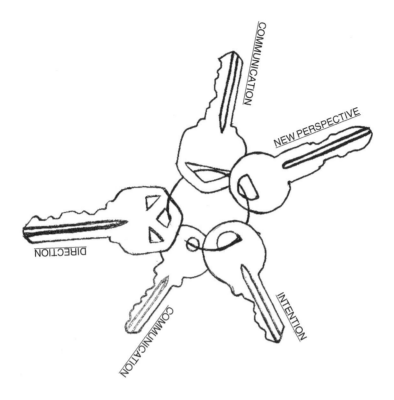

*Understanding*. This is a very important part of running game and is also typically overlooked by most.

As most people fail to understand another person's needs, their wants, and the things that someone may be lacking in their life, these things are important because they are a giveaway to what you'll need to know to work them over. Understanding how the game works is understanding how people work. There are a few things you must understand first. You must understand yourself before you try to understand anybody else. To understand yourself, you must know what it is you want and to know what you want. You must know who you are. Although it sounds funny and you might think you know who you are, but I assure you, this is actually more complicated than it sounds. We are made up by a series of events that we have been through in our lives along with the genes that are passed down to us from our parents. The thing that confuses us is our desire to belong, as everybody has this desire within them. It is the desire to belong that makes us feel as if we don't belong. This is what causes us to not know who we really are. And if we don't know who we really are, how would we know what we want?

Once you understand yourself and who you are along with what you want, you can start understanding other people.

When it comes to figuring yourself out, something I strongly suggest is to actually ask yourself the question you wish to have answered. Then try to answer the question and go through the motions of actually trying to figure the problem out. This sounds simple; however, you can find out a lot about yourself this way. Instead of thinking you already know something about yourself, just ask yourself. You may find out more about yourself than you thought.

The reason understanding is a key to game is so you may give other people what it is they want. The more you are able to understand people, the easier it will be to run game. People are drawn to people that understand them, their needs, and the things that drive them crazy. A lot of times, all you have to do to understand somebody is to simply listen to them talk, allowing them to tell you about themselves so they get a chance to feel as if you understand them.

*Direction.* You must project your game in the right direction, depending on what type of person you are dealing with, as everybody has their own goals and ideas of the direction they are trying to be heading in. You want to make sure the things you are talking about along with the ideas of different ways to achieve greatness are parallel to the ones of the person you wish to game in. This is because if you don't have the same views, then you may find out that this person would rather head in a new or different direction.

*Communication.* You must be able to communicate well with others, although it is important that you are able to talk to others. This key to game is based on being able to make others see where you are coming from and where you're going. This is so people can see your direction along with how you're going to get there. Communicating with others is very important, as it allows you a chance to show someone who you are or who you want them to think you are, as this type of communication is about relaying information to another.

*Intention*. Of the five keys to game, intention is the most important as it deals with your goals. Your intention will be the overall end result for which you intend to achieve. It's the reason why you are running game. This doesn't mean intention is your excuse for running game as to say you're running game because of your situation or current love-life scenario. No, this is about what you want to get out of running game, as your intentions for doing what you are doing is the most important key to game.

*Providing new perspective*. Although intention may be the most important, providing new perspective is the most powerful. It is very powerful because it changes the way a person is seeing things. This is key: if you want to be able to show direction, give understanding and communicate these to others to provide new perspective. You want to look for or create an opening for you to provide this new perspective for someone. Doesn't matter what creed or type of person you are dealing with, there will always be a way to provide new perspective. This doesn't mean that you go against the ideas that another person may have. It simply means you provide a new way to get there. This comes along with providing new thoughts for a person. This is what makes them feel differently about their current situation as people tend to start to feel trapped in the lifestyle or current situation they are in. They tend to feel as if there is no way to advance as they may feel even when they are at the top of their game. The person that may seem as if they have it all may seem like the person that doesn't need anything. This is why providing new perspective is so powerful because it can be used to draw in people that have it going on for themselves as they will now see a new way to advance or basically a solution to their problem that they aren't even aware they even had.

Providing new perspective is awesome because it has to do with changing another person's views or the way that they perceive things to be. Like I was saying earlier, you want to look for or create an opening. You can do this by doing something to make yourself stand out as different depending on the situation or what type of person you are looking to game in.

However, when you do something or say something to make yourself seem different, you want it to be in a passive type of way, subtle, not in a way that is so obvious.

This would be something simple just to create a question within someone's head which may lead to them asking you the question that they are throwing around in their head. This question will be the deciding factor as to whether they feel you are different than others or if you are the same. Whatever you decide to say, make sure it parallels with what you feel their direction is heading in. Meaning that you as a person would have the same goal in mind but with a different way to reach it.

This is what draws people in and makes them feel as if they need you in their life. As people will be naturally drawn to many things, however, new perspective not only makes people feel new with new thoughts and new hope, but it also gives new direction. This new direction will be given by you, the person that knows what direction to head on next to make it to the desired goal for which one intends to reach. As everybody loves brand new things, a brand-new perspective is one of them as you can imagine how awesome it would be to see things in a new way that would bring about new hope in your own life. This is why new perspective is such a powerful tool and is the basis that this whole book is based off of.

## Attention

Of all the things to offer someone, your attention is the one thing you don't want to give up. As all people will seek out attention in one way or another, it is attention that makes people feel important, loved, and cared about. This is why if you don't give people attention, they will surely find it somewhere else. However, I assure you the attention they get will not be from the person they want it from. The person they want attention from is the one person they can't get it from.

Just as you would desire to get someone's attention, it's only because you don't have it that you would want it so bad. Your attention is something you don't want to give out so easily because it places a higher value on your attention and your time. If you give up your attention and your time easily, then you will allow others to place a meager price on it as it may not be so valuable which is the exact opposite of what you want to be doing. Your goal should be to make yourself, your time, and your attention priceless.

When you do show attention to someone, make sure it's only to fulfill your own attention needs. As we all have needs, you will find out that you yourself have these very same needs that need to be fulfilled as well. When dealing with someone that gets plenty of attention, they will not be attention thirsty. This means if you want to get this person's attention, you will need to not show them any attention.

This is because these needs have been being met already, so by depriving them of your attention, people will start to want your attention as it's always the thing that people lack in their life that they will desire.

Attention is typically given by one person and received by another. It is almost untypical of two people to be giving each other the same amount of attention to one another. When this does occur, it is typically by two people that are newly in love with each other. The way attention typically works is one person will show their attention to one person while the other person just eats the attention up. It is my opinion that this is exactly how you keep a person's attention by not giving them yours.

## Being Select

Being select will draw people to you as well as keeping people that you don't want around you away from you. When you are select, people will work hard to try and be one of the people selected by you to be involved in your life. Being select also puts you in the position to be the selector that gets to pick and choose who that is let in your life. I remember when I was a kid, we would play different games while on recess in school. Lining up along the wall, there would be two predetermined captains that would pick out kids that they wanted on their team. One by one they would pick a player until there were one or two kids left. Can you remember what it felt like to be one of the kids to not get picked? I know today that if my skill level was on another level that I would have been picked.

I also know if I was accepted socially, I would have been picked. However, I learned quick that I needed to be one of the captains. This way, I would be the selector instead of being one of the kids that didn't get to play. Being one of the captains was a lot different. When I was captain, all the other kids had their hands up saying, "Pick me. Pick me." This technic carries over into my adult life today as I am the captain of my own team. I am the captain of my own team because I chose to be the selector by being select.

In

The goal is to win, and to do so, we must first stop losing by making a continuous decision to stop losing, to fight for one's self, not allowing others to take from us in one way or another. Now, for one's self to win doesn't mean someone else has to lose as this is a common misconception. However, as long as you're winning and you stay focused on winning and keep your motivations for the things you do based on winning in every way, you can be sure that you can stay winning as people sometimes forget that by not winning you are losing.

This is because eventually all your losses end up all adding up to one big loss which makes you one big loser. So every time you are taken from or taken advantage of, you are losing. Every time someone takes something from you, whether its physical or mental, it's a loss, and you are losing. You may not look at this loss as anything major, so you might allow such a meager loss to just slide. But what happens when you take a small loss here then another small loss after that? Then you let another small loss just slide not thinking anything of it until it all adds up.

The answer is you end up taking one big loss, and in the end, it seems as if you feel you are one big loser. In a book called *Winning Against All Odds* written by Dr. Don Shorter, he talks a lot about patterning. He says winning is about patterning. We must pattern our lives out to win, as a person that is constantly losing has almost set themselves up to do so through patterning themselves to do so. As when a person does the same thing over and over, you may start to see a pattern emerge. This pattern may be the key in guessing what this person's next move will be. Well, the same goes for winning or losing.

In the book *Winning Against All Odds*, Dr. Don Shorter says that winning is about cutting out **chances.** The reason for this is because when you take chances, you take the risk of a possible loss, and these are the possible losses we need to eliminate.

He also gives an example of how desperate people are to win at everything in life. He gives the example of how people go to casinos with the goal of winning in mind. Now these people rarely win. And this is because they leave their chance of winning up to the casinos because these games the casinos provide are based on chance. What these casinos are really selling are dreams of what could be.

These casinos have a tactic that works every time as they draw people in for one thing and actually give their customers something else. These casinos don't make any promises, but their commercials are sure persuading enough to get people down there playing these games every night and day. These casinos use the same tactic that we will be using to run game, not by promising anything but by making ourselves out to look like the solution to problems through selling hope to a person that has no hope, by selling dreams to the person that has no dreams, by showing care to the person that doesn't care anymore, by loving the unlovable even for just a moment. Our tactic is based on feeding the needy.

We will also be playing on the desires of others by providing a new path toward winning the things that they desire because people desire so much more than just money. They desire to win in one way or another. People want to win, and we need to be able to make people want to take that chance with us as we may feel their desire to win by making them feel as if with us they have a chance at winning.

## Game Recognize Game

*Game recognize game* is all about making yourself familiar with the game strategies and technics. This is because you want to know game when you see it. And others will too, not so much in your strategy but in your technic. Although people may see through your strategy, it is typically through your technic that your game-like mentality will be exposed. If you look at it like this, our strategy will be the place you're trying to get to. Your technic will be the avenue in which you wish to travel to get there.

This is why people's game is so easy to see through and unsuccessful because they are obvious in their strategy as they fail to step their game up. Much like the strategies given in this book, they will need to be forever changing.

In the effort to step your game up, although these may be good basic strategies, they will need to be altered from time to time in the effort to step your game up. If you do not alter or change your strategies and technic, you will find these to both seem obvious to another player.

This is why they say *game recognize game* as you will to when you see another person trying to play you for stupid. Recognizing game amongst other players will also draw a player to you as other players are attracted to other players because it seems to put the two on the same level or page as one another.

However, it is not going to be in the same way as you may think as this type of attraction won't last for long and is more of a coworker-type relationship.

## Everybody Uses Everybody

Everybody and everything in this world uses something or somebody to survive as it can be seen all over, especially in nature. As the flowers use the sun to grow, some of the biggest creatures here on earth like the whale that eats seals and the seals that eat the fish and the fish that eats the plankton off of the corals. Well, humans use each other as well, and it's surprisingly just as vicious as some of the whales or sharks that attack the sea lions as humans carry the capacity to take a person's heart away along with their thoughts and much, much more.

People have the capacity to strip another, their belongings, their thoughts, the way they feel about themselves, the way they feel about others to the point their thought process is altered, and so on. Of all the animals on this planet, animals like the wolf seem to show similar technics as humans as they travel in packs so that they can use each other to hunt food. They also use each other to keep warm. However, when it comes down to it, they show no care with attacking each other if need be.

This is where the saying dog-eat-dog world comes from, as typically in nature one species of animal typically eats another species to survive. Well, the wolf has no problem with attacking and eating another wolf once it's dead, and this is eerily similar to how humans are. Although humans don't typically eat other humans, they tend to take from another human to the point of utter exhaustion. Another similarity to humans is explained well in a saying I once heard, and it goes like this: "In a pack of wolves, if one dog is mean, they will all be mean." As to say you're not going to find a pack of wolves that is made up by three mean dogs and two nice dogs. As humans are the same way, if one guy is mean in that group, the whole group will typically be mean as well.

As everybody takes from everybody and everybody uses somebody, there will be many people that try to take from you in many ways, all for their own self-advancement. Although I wouldn't ever advise you to go out there and start taking from people in an effort to hurt people so that you won't be taken from, but I am going to suggest that you realize that everybody takes from somebody even when you give to somebody the feelings you take away from. The good deed you just did are a gift. And so although I don't suggest your goal should be to take from people, I do say it is okay, as we are all taking something from somebody to survive as many people will get caught up on trying to be a good person. This is a good thing as well as a bad thing. This is because it's good to be a good person as people are definitely attracted to good people. However, it is the goal of this topic—to show that in a dog-eat-dog world, things like feelings of being a user are similar to feelings of being a loser or any other type of feelings, but feelings of being a user will keep you from taking the things that you need in life. As everybody takes from somebody, you may be required to do the same so that you can survive. It is my opinion that this is just part of nature and is a necessary evil needed for human advancement.

When you take something from somebody in one way or another, you want to show appreciation for what they have done for you because when you take from a person then you just discard them like they were used. It will anger people to the point they feel they need to do something to hurt you back or to take from you just as you have taken from them. This is definitely not a good way to go about gaining things as your main goal should always be getting and keeping the hearts and minds of others, as this can be lifted at as the gift that keeps giving as you will always gain more from a long-lasting relationship of any kind than you will in a short one.

# Chapter 4

# Value Driven

> One must not hold one's self so divine as to be unwilling occasionally to make improvements in one's creations.
> —Ludwig van Beethoven

IF YOU WANT TO DRAW people to you, then you must be willing to work on one's self as who you are as a person, as people are attracted to people that show good qualities and traits. Things like loyalty, compassion, good morals, work ethic, and so on, have become forgotten as these are some of the most basic traits that were taught to us or most of us as we were kids. They tend to be looked down upon as a weakness by others that only wish to take from us.

On one side of the spectrum, we have correct principles. These are the principles most of us live by today: living correctly driven lives that are based upon getting a good job and finding a good partner to live our lives out with, being good and loyal to your partner. And on the other side of the spectrum, we have people that chose to live by the street and the rules and regulations that govern their lives. This is why this book combines the two so that, as people, we may live value-driven lives as we should, but it also points out some of the games others will play on you in the effort to gain off of you as people have become hungry enough to where they are willing to play on any and every aspect of life for their benefit. If we take a look at where we all came from, it's easy to see how this could happen. From the moment we are born, we know no right, we know no wrong, but as we start to grow, our parents start teaching us what they want us to know on a very basic level. They tell us to not touch the stove and so on. As we start to get a little bit older, they start teaching us ways to be and ways not to be. You may remember your parents telling you to be nice to your brother or sister. Maybe they told you to not be mean to the family cat or something like that.

I remember always being told to share with my friends or my brother constantly. As we start to get a little bit older to the age, we can start taking care of ourselves. We may be left alone at times. It is at this point we start to establish feelings and desires of all types. We start attempting to figure out just who we are, and as we do so, we start looking to others our age for a sense of belonging. Whether we are selected by others to belong in their social group depends on a variety of personality likes and dislikes.

The more we start to feel as if we belong to some sort of social group, the more detached we become to anything other than making sure that we fit among this group. The ways of the people in this group seem to have a profound effect on us and how we will act for the most part of our lives. When we become eighteen years old, the world considers us as an adult and says that we are capable of making our own decisions. This is the point where we get a taste of what it's like to be an adult.

We have bills to pay and relationships that typically end up badly most of the time. We become so overwhelmed with the stresses that life brings to where we have no time to actually think about ourselves and our dreams that we once had for ourselves. Our lives become complexed in every way as we struggle to just make it in life. As we are sent out into the world, we have to work off of what we know. For the most part, all we do know is what has been taught to us in school and by our parents which isn't much, seeing how our parents are typically caught up with their own lives, and the things we really want to ask them won't be answered in the manner needed.

As we begin to try and figure out things for ourselves, we may mix and match different ideas in the hopes of being successful.

But in many cases, we lack knowledge of human relations, and this is where we go wrong. For an example, as people, we typically look to find a partner to share our lives with, and even if we aren't looking for someone, somehow or another, we do look to other people to provide some of our needs in life. This is why it is so important we work on our human relations so that not only will we be more aware of the things we need to do to get the things out of others, but we will also be more aware of the things others will try to do in an effort to do the same.

Human relations is very important and is one of the most basic necessities that school or our parents taught us. We are just expected to know things based upon our life experience. This life experience may cost us a lifetime of pain and regret and, not to mention, lots and lots of hard-earned money. This isn't to say that someone should know how basic interactions with others work. It is more like how to work others within using what we know about other people and how exactly they work to our advantage so that, in a sense, we can have others working in our favor doing the things that we want them to do for our own self-betterment. This is why there is so much to having game. It is a lifestyle for most, and for those that don't choose to live the lifestyle required to harness the skill of running game tend to get the brunt of the harshness that may be brought about from those that do.

People are attracted to the good traits **that** a person has, not just in the hopes to take advantage of them. But because people want people with good traits and values in their life as well, that is why this chapter focuses on adding proper traits and values to your game without putting yourself in the position to be taken advantage of. We will also be exploring feelings and how they can be a good thing or a bad thing for one's self. Values and traits are very important because they give us a good core or foundation to start off, as a person that starts their life off of a foundation based around game and playing games will not be fully successful in running game because that will be all they know without ever adding the other qualities and traits to their game because they will seem as backward traits and values.

However, a person that starts their life or foundation based off of good qualities and traits has a much better background and chance for success both in life and in running game. This is because if you have a good quality set of morals and standards to base your life off of, it will be easy to add game strategies and technics to your skill set. It is the person that has a game-style upbringing that has put themselves in the position to play themselves short of their full potential.

This is because when you take a person who only knows game strategies and technics and you try to add proper principles into their life, they will typically see these principles as nothing but weaknesses. It is hard for this type of person to see anything as being beneficial unless it goes with the game that they already know. To this type of person running game isn't just a skill set that they add to their person and in who they are, it is the exact material that makes them who they are.

On the other hand, the person that starts their foundation off of a good solid foundation based upon living a good life in every aspect is looking to add game to their skill set and will be much more successful. It also helps for a person to know what ways should be looked upon as right or wrong, good or bad, in the proper manner instead of learning the backward manner that the game can sometimes bring. This is also a good way to build a person from the ground up. To do so, first we must start with ourselves. So throughout this chapter, we will be comparing proper principles to game-principles strategies and technics. First, we'll start with loyalty as loyalty is a very sought-out and desired quality. It is also this quality that can be very harmful to a person in many ways.

Like I explained earlier, everything starts with self. In order for you to be loyal to anything, you must first be loyal to yourself.

Being loyal to yourself would mean that you never cheat yourself of the different possibilities that life has to offer you. You put yourself first and foremost above all others, your needs, your wants, and most of all, yourself. This will typically help you to want to be around people that are loyal to you as well. Loyalty is a trait that so many people of all walks of life lack, and this is also why it is so desirable.

Every good quality and trait you have will make you more valuable, as a person that has no good qualities and traits may be seen as a person of little to no value to others. Once you are loyal to yourself, you may begin to offer loyalty to others. However, I ask the question *why*. It is my opinion that the only time you should be loyal to others is if they are loyal to you. Although a person may appear to be loyal, it doesn't mean that they really are. It will be up to you to take in all information known about a person and make this decision for yourself.

It is my opinion that, more than being loyal to yourself or others, there is a set of principles that are much more important to be loyal to. However, these principles are or should be centered around one's self. These principles include things like loving yourself before and above any other person, trusting yourself above any other person, respecting yourself above any other person, never allowing another person to hold anything above our heads as this may be done by others when we put ourselves in the position to where we need anything from someone else that we can't get from another person. It is my opinion that as a person you should sit down with yourself and ask yourself. What things do you require from other people? Then I suggest you figure out a way to eliminate these things to the point that you don't need them anymore because you have them. In another form, if need be, kinda like a back-up plan.

On the following page, I have included a diagram that is split into four parts. I call this a strength-and-weakness grid. This strength-and-weaknesses grid is based upon traits that you may or may not have. This grid is meant to strengthen who you are as a person. In the top left corner, it says the word *strength*. This would be where you list your strengths you have within the different traits you have or would like to have. In the box on the right, it says the word *weakness*. This is where you list your weaknesses. In the bottom left side of the grid, it says problems solved by strengths. You would list the problems that may be solved by the strengths that you have.

The box on the bottom right says *problems created by weakness*, and of course, you list the problems created by your weakness. The goal of this exercise is to see what traits you would like to harness so that they can be used to your advantage as a strength and not a weakness.

# CRAIG A. MASSEY

HUSTLE N GAME

STRENGTH/WEAKNESS GRID

<u>TRAITS</u>

| <u>STRENGTH</u> | <u>WEAKNESS</u> |
|---|---|
| <u>PROBLEMS SOLVED BY STRENGTH</u> | <u>PROBLEMS SOLVED BY WEAKNESS</u> |

The strength-and-weakness grid is an awesome tool that can be used to your advantage as it helps you see what traits give off strengths or weakness. If we take a step back and look at ourselves, not in the mirror, not within thought, not even within our hearts, but we really take a step back and look at who we really are at the core of our very soul. You will see that our feelings aren't us. Our brains aren't us. Neither is the house we live in or our jobs, but we are spiritual creatures, and we are only here on earth for a small amount of time.

Once we step back and look at things in this manner, you will see it is very easy to alter the very material that makes you who you are.

By this I mean, you may start to realize that you make you you. And any traits and qualities you wish to have, you may certainly make them a reality by simply harnessing these qualities and traits and make them your own. Some of the qualities and traits that people living their whole lives based off of game strategies and technics have inserted these strategies into the qualities that they have as a person which only makes them a weaker person without any good traits about themselves at all. Like a person that doesn't trust anyone, it makes them paranoid, or a person that doesn't love anyone, it makes them unlovable themselves. This is why I can't stress it enough to make sure you build yourself a good solid foundation to work off of by inserting good qualities and traits within your character and in who you are as a person.

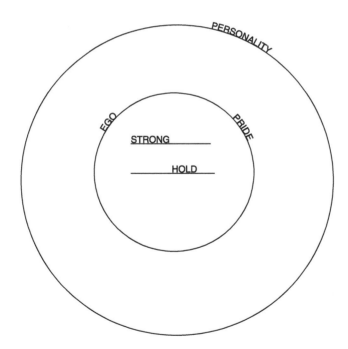

This is why I have included what I call the *circle of life*. The circle of life consists of two circles. The most inner circle is for your qualities and traits, and the outer circle is where your skills, strategy, technic, and your personality reside. I have done this not only so that you can see that you can put anything you want into your circle of life but also so that you may see the difference between the two qualities and traits or strategy and technic because the two are very different, and you don't want to get them confused.

# Chapter 5

# Selling Dreams

> Where there is no strife there is decay; the
> mixture that is not shaken decomposes.
> —Heraclitus

GAME CAN BE LOOKED AT as a business, and you are in the business of selling dreams and gaming hearts.

The first thing you must do in any business is to determine your image. You can do this by writing up a self-evaluation sheet that will include your good traits along with your bad traits in the hopes to get rid of the bad traits that you have. You may also write up a strength-and-weakness grid and look to find ways to make some of your weakness your strongest point about yourself. You may add or subtract to your strength and weakness along with your qualities and traits to determine your image.

It is important that you know your person's needs as this will be what attracts them to you. When you are looking to provide someone with the things they need to draw them to you, it is important that you must realize you are solving people's problems, and you want to do so without creating new ones.

This is also why it is important to invest good qualities and traits within who you are as a person. Typically, this is what a person needs in their life, person with good qualities and traits, but they also help you to be able to solve problems without creating new problems. It is also very important to work hard to get people to say good things about you as half of your business will come by referral from another person.

This is why you want to work hard to get people to say good things about you, eliminating those that hurt your image as your image is everything, as your image will be based upon what you put out there for other people to see. You don't want other people putting a bad image out there for you. Your goal should be to get people to be talking good about you. This is what they call in the business world *creating a positive buzz*. This is where you get as many people within your circle to be talking good about you which will bring clients, and clients are the most important people to any business. It is also very important for you to know your competition and find ways to use them to your advantage as there are many people that will consider themselves competition, and you should too until you find a way to use them to your advantage. There are many ways to do this, and it is up to you to find these ways out.

As you modify your strategies as knowledge and power is gained, there are many ways to be able to tell when a person is lying to you, especially when you have had continued contact with that person in particular as you will be able to factor in facial expressions, body language, and their tendencies. However, generally people that are lying will have long drawn-out stories that are in-depth in detail.

This is because they are attempting to get you to believe their story, and they need every bit of information to get you to believe their story. It is typical of people that are lying to avoid confrontation until they feel they have drummed up a story big enough to be believable. People that are lying typically will repeat themselves or the question asked to them. They do this because it gives them time to think up a lie. They will also act as if they don't understand the question.

This is typically a strategy used to get around the question as they act as if they don't understand the question itself. People that are lying will typically use words like *them* or they oppose to words like *I* or *me*. This is because the person lying is trying to find ways to take the blame off of themselves. A liar will also try to fast-talk you. This is where a person talks so fast that you can barely understand them. This is done in an effort to confuse you and to get you to stop asking them questions as the person lying will attempt to get you to feel as if you may be stressing them out to the point of frustration.

People will also give themselves away with their body language. This is due to the fact that when a person is thinking up a lie, they can't focus on their body language.

So a person may act fidgety or pace around sometimes. They may shake at times as this is a trait of a nervous person.

The sound in their voice may be broken up when they speak as this is due to stress on the body due to the thought of exposure of the pending lie. When a person is lying, they tend to have poor posture, as this shows how they feel on the inside due to the shame that they feel. A person that is lying will usually look downward when they are lying as opposed to looking up.

The best way to catch a liar up in their lie is to allow them to hang themselves by simply allowing them to tell you their story all the way through. It is best to not be trying to point out things that you feel are a lie or fictitious until their story is complete. Calmly take in all the information provided then make your own assessment on what you feel is true and what is not. As anytime you attempt to pick apart someone's story, it leaves room for argument. At this point, you should not be looking to argue as you are looking for facts to prove what you feel is truth.

In fact, sometimes it is a strategy of the liar to look to blow things out of proportion so that they don't get found out, as typically a blow-out fight ends the argument.

Another strategy of the liar is to attempt to confuse you as anytime someone is looking to explain themselves it should be a clear and straightforward, basic answer.

People that attempt to confuse you do so because it is in their best interest to keep you confused as a person that is confused will typically believe anything that you tell them. So don't look too deep into the story and start thinking too much as this may be part of the liar's strategy to confuse you.

# Control

When a person likes you, control will be something that is a dead giveaway to their true intentions as a person that likes you truly will look to give you control as opposed to the person that doesn't really like you. Now this may seem silly, but I assure you, a person that gives you control over the activities that you are doing control over the situation and generally control over the aspects in your own activities that the two of you are doing will be the person that truly likes you and wants you to be happy, and this is why they want you to make your own decisions as they are happy to follow your lead.

However, it is the person that looks to take control over you, the situation and all of the things possible, that will have an ulterior, or should I say, interior motive as people that look to take control of you and the situation will be only looking to take from you. When someone is looking to use you, the first thing they look for is control over you. When a person has control over you, they will also have control over your possessions as well.

Control over another person is gained three different ways. The first is self-will. This is where you offer to give or take something away from a person in the effort to get them to want to do what it is you want. This is a strategy that can be used without too much effort as the basic goal is to get a person to want to do things for you willingly. This is also the basic idea behind the next two ways, and those two are love and fear. It is typical of people that are trying to control you to use both technics. Love and fear—when one fails, they will try another. This can best be seen in a person that may be kind and loving one minute then mean and uncaring the next.

This is because when love didn't work, they knew fear would. Love is desired by all, and this is the reason it is used so often by people to get the things they want as nothing is free, so the thing that you want will cost you. However, a person that loves another person will give with an endless amount of abundance.

When a person tries to control you, this should be an obvious sign that they are looking to take from you. Although they may seem as if they care about you or may even love you, but one sure way to know if these people really do care is by control. The person that looks to control you does not care about anyone but themselves.

Control is a key element in using people as it is this control that is used in getting people to do whatever you want them to do. Another word for control can be *power of persuasion* as this persuasion is very important to the user, as they will do things just to show off their power over you, such as telling you to do things that are counterproductive to your success then sitting back and laughing about it as they point this action out to a possible peer or friend just to show off their power over you. So be aware of the person that looks to control you or persuade you to do things that you typically wouldn't do.

## Titles

Stay away from titles as people will try and use titles to make you feel as if you have a position or basically a job. This is done so that they can hold you accountable for fulfilling the duties required to uphold the position. Titles are a way for people to control you, and these types of people that look to put a label or title on you are easy to point out as they will be the ones to put a label on you early on in the relationship of any sort. It doesn't matter what this label may be. It could be brother, sister, boyfriend, girlfriend, best friend. The list goes on. There are many titles that come with certain responsibilities.

The type of person that will place these responsibilities on you without you even applying for the position are typically players that are looking to form a team. This is why they are looking to assign you a position on their team. Another reason you want to avoid labels is because, by doing so, you allow these people to assign a value on you as every label or title will have a value given to that position. When you allow people to put a label or title on you, sometimes you may find yourself trying to hold on to a title or label that you never even signed up for or never really wanted in the first place.

Titles make people feel as if they're someone special as all people live for purpose and reason to live. As these titles may make you feel like you belong to a group or team, do not get caught up in allowing someone to give you a position on their team, placing these titles on you. This is exactly what they are doing. If you're going to consider yourself as a member on any team, it is my opinion that you should be the captain of your own team.

## Expectations

The greater the expectation, the greater your level of disappointment.

This means, the more you expect from people, the more disappointed you will be. The only thing you can really expect from a person is for them to be exactly who they are.

For an example, you can expect for a good man, so do just that. Be a good man. You can expect a bitch, so do just that. Be a bitch. You can expect a good woman, so do just that. Be a good woman. You can expect the lame or be lame.

Having expectations for what you expect people to be like or what you expect them to do will leave you disappointed every time, so do not let yourself down by expecting others to do the things they say or to be the people they say they are. Expectations are typically tied to a label as one will try to place a label on someone in the effort to set expectations on them. It is my opinion that you should not put yourself in the position to be disappointed by others; however, I think it is better if you make people feel as if you expect a lot out of them as to say you have high expectations that you wish for them to hold up to, although you may not expect much from them so that you're not let down. At the same time, it is these high expectations they must live up to if they wish to be in your life because if they're not living up to these expectations, then they're not up to your standards for what you're expecting from them.

This is a great way to draw people in, believe it or not, because people are drawn to people that make them a better person, as people tend to feel that a person makes them better as a person as opposed to a person that doesn't have high standards for them to live up to. Besides, a person that allows another person to be sloppy and foolish is in fact just that foolish. This is because when you don't expect much of a person, you don't get much from a person. Placing high expectations on a person is a way of keeping a person in check, so to speak. This is because it causes a person to check themselves to the point that they are making sure that they are doing everything they're supposed to be doing.

Placing verbal expectations on a person will also make yourself a better person as well. This is because when you tell a person what you expect out of them, it puts you, yourself, in the position to check yourself, as far as making sure that you are holding yourself up to the expectations that you are holding others to as well. It is very important to make sure that the people in your life are aware of what you expect from them so that they can provide you with what it is that you expect them to provide you with. This can be money or possessions, but typically we would be referring to qualities and traits that one desires in a person.

These qualities and traits lead to actions as people with poor qualities and traits typically have poor actions. Just as people with poor actions showcase poor qualities and traits as a person, it is a person's actions that make them who they are because it seems, as people, we aren't typically judged by what we do, only one time.

However, we are judged by others on our repeated actions and things that we do over and over again. This is because when you do something over and over, it gets to the point that people feel that's just who you are.

However, you do not want to allow people the opportunity to do something over and over if the thing they are doing is based upon poor actions and poor performance. When you are looking to set high expectations on them, you will want to let them know right away that their performance along with their actions will not be tolerated. As their actions are below what is expected of them, especially when it comes to respect, as anytime a person does something that shows any form of disrespect, you must do something drastic to make sure that the other person knows to never ever try to do anything disrespectful.

This is because disrespect is one of the few things that once tolerated one time is looked at as being acceptable a second time. It is very important to not give people chances because it seems once they have gotten one chance, they may feel as if there will be another chance and another chance to disrespect you once again, and respect is very important, especially if you are looking to put expectations on a person as it is the person that does not respect you that will not be looking to uphold themselves to any expectations of a person that they don't respect.

As all people have the desire to be great, it will be the high expectations that you make them hold up to that will draw a person in as it is this high expectation you place on them that will make them feel as if they're part of something greater than themselves and the typical lifestyle that they are used to. Of course, it is also good to place high expectations on another so that you don't have to put up with anything lesser than you don't want to. So we now know that it is a good thing to place high expectations on others as it draws them in and makes not only those around you better people, but it also makes you a better person.

As far as actually expecting any person to be a certain way or to respect you without reason, don't expect it because you will be let down every time, as you must expect a person to be just who they are. A snake is always going to be a snake, and a pit bull will always be a pit bull. A snake is going to hiss, and a pit bull is going to bark. So what makes a person think that they can change that? I don't know, but what I do know is by placing expectations on people, they will be drawn to you; however, actually expecting anything from them will let you down every time.

## Chapter 6

# It's All About You

> What I do today is important because I'm
> exchanging a day of my life for it.
>
> —Hugh Milligan

EVERYBODY HAS SOMETHING THEY CENTER their life on. There are many different things that a person may center their life around. Some people center their lives around money while others may be friend centered or maybe self-centered. These centers are very important as they can tell you so much about a person.

For an example, a person that is friend centered will typically care way too much about what their friends think about them. This will also be the person that tends to keep up with the Joneses. This type of person will be happy and feel good when their friends are around. As long as their friends are happy, then they're happy. Their friends are where they are strongest. This type of person may be hurt easily by someone they consider to be a friend. This person would be a good friend to have and is anything but self-centered.

A person that is money centered will base all their actions around the getting and finding of money. Money gives them their power, and without it, they tend to feel powerless. Their money gives them a sense of self-worth. Money tends to run their lives, and it will become the only thing they are interested in.

A person that is self-centered will be all about themselves. They like to hear others talk about them as this solidifies their thoughts they already have, which are typically all about themselves. As this type of person only thinks about themselves and how they can gain possessions only for themselves, these types of people only include others when in some way or another it is beneficial to themselves. They are full of themselves in every way. They don't take criticism well, and so on.

These centers give you an idea of who someone is without them even telling you anything about themselves.

All you have to do is figure out what you think a person centers their life around, and you will typically know so much about the person once you know a person's center. You will know what is important to them, where they get their strengths, and what their weaknesses are. You will know what types of things they believe in, what they like, and what they don't like.

To determine a person's center, all you need to do is look to figure out where you believe they spend their time, as it will be where a person spends their time that will show what types of things they care about or are interested in. A person's center can be seen in the clothes they wear, the way they walk or carry themselves, the type of vehicle they drive, or even how they treat themselves or their friends. All these things may factor in to help you determine what their center is or basically the thing they center their lives on.

This is a very helpful technic that can be used to help you find out information about a person without them ever saying a word to you. It is good to know what types of things a person is interested in when you decide to talk to this person as having the same interests as another person is, typically a good way to create a situation where this person will be drawn to you. Keep in mind, there are many, many centers besides the ones that I named off. There are people that are drug centered, family centered, material centered, sex centered, work centered. The list goes on and on as this technic is so helpful because as people change, so do their centers. Using this technic, you won't find yourself getting stuck on what you think you already know about a person as being true, if you always look to evaluate what their center is or seems to be at the current time and place.

## House Cats and Wild Cats

It seems there is definitely a difference between house cats and wildcats as house cats seem to be nice and will walk right up to you while wildcats will run from you, and if you try to catch one, they will scratch you.

Although both house cats and wild cats have the ability to scratch you, wildcats live in an environment where they are required to act and react in such a manner for their protection as they act as they need to in order to survive in the harsh environment they live in.

While house cats aren't subjected to the harsh realities that life can sometimes bring, house cats are a lot nicer and are similar to the type of people that have lived a somewhat sheltered life through having jobs and families that take them in under their wing in their time of need, through living value-driven lives where their morals are still intact and they have not been tarnished by the harsh realities that life sometimes brings.

On the other side of the spectrum, there are many people that never had jobs or the support of their families.

If there ever was someone to look out for them, it was by someone that was simply putting them up on game. Of course, the word *game* refers to the word *knowledge*, and it is through this knowledge of human relations that people have been able to find other ways to get the things they need or want. These people have become hardened by the streets, much like the alley cat. These types of people have forgotten their morals and left behind any real chance at advancing in their game.

## Level of Operation

You want to build yourself up as a person as you are building up your game and gaining knowledge. You can do this simply by taking what has been proven to work for others and building off of it by either adding or subtracting qualities and traits and combining them with the right skill set as practice doesn't make perfect, but perfect practice makes perfect. So you must practice these strategies in perfect form if you want to gain anything from them. Once you start practicing these strategies in perfect form, you will be able to alter them to your liking in the effort to eventually step your game up.

When you step your game up to where you're operating on a higher level, meaning above the rest of the people in your immediate circle, you must change your circle of people that you surround yourself with so that the people around you are the type of people that are operating on the same level or close to the same level as you are. If you don't, then you will find yourself still playing off of the original set of principles, knowledge, and all the traditional expectations of the person that is considered to be up on game.

However, when you are operating on a higher level but functioning around lower-level people, you actually put yourself in the position to be played or taken advantage of, I assure you, and it is the goal of this book to get more people operating on a higher level and to step their game up so that there is more and more people with the skill set and mind-set needed to match the others that have already been stepping their game up and advancing as knowledge and power is gained. We as people need to stay committed to forever stepping our game up both from within ourselves and in the field where these games are played through the art of game.

The problem is people have become satisfied with the strategies and technics that they have learned already, so they fail to stay forever stepping their game up. These strategies and technics are typically gathered here and there through a lifetime of distrust and hardship mostly through word of mouth coming from others, and their information is scattered and forgotten and a lot of times not even reliable information. This has left people in the position to where they win sometimes and lose others. This is simply due to the fact that most people are lacking any real knowledge or skill needed to be what is called game tight.

By you yourself altering small flaws that are written into the game, you can actually rewrite the game itself, turning the game on its head and altering the game to your liking. After all, it is your game. How you run your game will be left up to you. The game that you are running on others needs to leave people feeling like they are winning in the situation or, in other words, like they are advancing, although you want to be sure that overall you are the victor or the one gaining the most off of the situation or relationship.

As people are constantly tearing each other down, you will be left to make a choice. Are you going to choose to tear down those that tear you down, or are you going to choose to build up those that build you up, or are you going to do both? If you choose to do both, then how will you ever know which people are which? The problem is it's nearly impossible to do both at the same time. This is why you see the separation among the people that are all about building each other up and tearing each other down. **It's** almost like they feel they can't operate among each other when really in the end they are forced to do so anyway, each and every day.

This is why it is important to keep stepping your game up and to stay changing your technic as knowledge and power are gained, turning those that only desire to take from us into the stepping stones that will help us to advance.

As we already know, everyone that decides to reach out to us only does so for their own self-betterment in the hopes to advance themselves. It doesn't matter which technic they choose to use or which route they look to take. It is my opinion that just as everyone else is in it for their own selfish needs that you should do the same. However, it's not always what a person does but how they do it, and I think, whatever you do, you will be able to accomplish your goals easily. If you make sure to operate with a certain level of finesse that will draw the things to you that you desire, it won't matter if you want to take advantage of those that are only looking to take an advantage of you or if you look to build up those that build you up as operating with a certain level of finesse will always attract the things that you want. This way if you are attracting the things that you want, you can't go wrong unless you are desiring unhealthy things for yourself.

As it is very typical of people to try to act as if they may be a friend to you when they are anything but a friend, you may find people trying to act as if they are trustworthy when they are not. They are nothing but snakes in the grass, and at times, it may seem as if these snakes in the grass are getting the upper hand. This is how you know it is time to step your game up as these snakes in the grass are lame and typically almost obvious, and I assure you that you don't have to be a snake yourself in order to see them in the tall grass.

The fact of the matter is that the snakes in the grass are always looking to get over on somebody because they feel if they don't get over on you that you will get over on them. This mind-set is typical and is the very reason they are left to not advance as they try to take before they are taken from. These people leave behind a world of possibilities and actually cut the relationship short because they are so selfish they fail to be able to take full advantage of all the perks that a relationship of any kind has to offer.

The idea itself is the seed that actually needs others to help it grow in the effort to change people's way of viewing things as ideas die off when underpowered by the masses to actually bring a new to life. Just as this game was created through small changes made to protect the art of game, it will be through small changes that we need to instill in others so that we can continue to evolve as it is these snakes in the grass aren't going anywhere with their game as they have suddenly seemed to stop evolving and growing and stepping their game up. They use the same lame strategy and technic of stealth.

The overall goal should be to advance yourself. The problem is the way that people are going about doing, so the only real way that you will see advancement and change is through working on yourself by working on yourself, I mean adding to your knowledge, such as a person that has no knowledge of game activities and why they are played should take the time to harness the capabilities behind them. Just as the person that has no knowledge of the possibilities that living value-driven lives can bring for you to grow, you must stay ever changing because if you're not changing, then you're not growing. The only way to stay ever changing is to keep gaining knowledge and to use it to your advantage and to use it to grow as this is what stepping your game up is about, growing with knowledge and going places that you have never been both physically and mentally. The game will always be the same game. If you do not change, then neither will the game. This is why I say that you can change the game because you can do it by changing yourself.

If you're always using the same mind frame to get your goals accomplished, it's because your goals haven't changed, and if your goals haven't changed, then neither have you. Therefore, you haven't grown at all. There is nothing you can do about changing other people except to change yourself and watch how others will follow. A common misconception that I see very commonly is that people seem to feel that they need to be doing the same things as others so that they will have something in common, and in the end, they end up sharing the one thing that they didn't want to have in common, and that is failure.

Game is all about manipulation and being able to manipulate other people into doing what you want them to do. You do this by convincing another person that it is in their own best interest to do so. You are looking to manipulate their mind into seeing things the way that you want them to see them. Some people become so good at this that they actually start manipulating their own minds into seeing things the way that they want to see them, shutting out all truth to the point that they believe their own lies.

This type of manipulation may be helpful to some such as a football player that is in pain. However, it is not typically a good thing for someone to be looking to manipulate themselves and is an even worse hardship to be doing so and not even recognize it. Manipulation can be looked at as a wall that is built up around the truth blocking but any sense of reason or truth. The manipulator would be the person that sit on top of the wall explaining to the people or person on the ground what it is they see. Although the person on the ground may have an idea of what's on the other side of the wall, they never truly know as the person on the ground has become naive to the ways of the manipulator.

The manipulator may draw in-depth pictures on the wall in an effort to show what's on the other side of the wall in an effort to control their mind. Manipulators feed off of fear and lies as they attempt to bend the truth so far that you wouldn't even dream of being able to wrap your mind around what's really going on. Sometimes the truth can be stretched out so far. It must seem that only the truly naive will believe it. This is why it is also the job of the manipulator to seek out the naive in the effort to work their manipulative ways on them.

This makes the manipulator's job much easier and will help to build the confidence of the manipulator. The more and more they are able to get people to believe their lies and are able to get people to see things the way that they are seeing things or the way they want them to. As the manipulators' confidence grow, they begin to become bolder and start to take things to new heights as they become a master manipulator. Although game can sometimes be all about manipulating the mind, I do not suggest it as it is fake and only a strategy used by the lowest as lying and cheating is the lowest form that a person can operate on in an effort to get the things they want from people. I like to refer to this as running drama as opposed to running game. Running drama is when someone creates a rather poisonous atmosphere through lies and making up stories that just aren't true, all in an effort to get you to do the things they want you to do. This is different than running game. As when running game, you look to gain the heart and mind in the effort to get what you want from people. Or you gain the heart and mind so that you can get people to do what it is you want. Running drama is much different, but people use it in the effort to get the same result.

People that are running drama will make up stories and lie constantly just to get you to do what they want. There are many different strategies and technics that are used when running drama, and they are all very different than running game. The reason that I will be talking about them in this book is because it is something to look for as a relationship of any sort that is built off of running drama will be the most toxic.

## String Along

The string-along technic works like this: when someone feels that they may need you in their life but they are all too caught up in the life they are living on the side, they will attempt to keep you around by stringing you along. This technic is lame, and it is run by lame people, so I do not condone this type of behavior. The person that is running the string-along technic does not care for or about you, and this is why they are stringing you along. They string you along because they care about what you can do for them. They do not care about you as a person.

The person that looks to string you along simply does not care enough to spend the time that may be desired by someone, although they will occasionally make meager or small attempts to try and show you they care for you.

This is in the effort to keep you around. Do not be mistaken as these people are only looking to keep you around for their own selfish needs. This person may do things like call or text you out of the blue asking for a favor. Once you respond back and tell them you will do the favor, they will then say that they don't no longer need the favor they just asked you for. This is done so that a person may check on you and see where you stand, as a person that is mad or don't want anything to do with someone will not do the favor. This favor was just used to see if you are still on their team.

It is typical of the person that is doing this to have been absent or MIA which is missing in action. The person that running this drama is doing so based off of the feelings or emotions that you have for them.

As relationships are built and kept through continuous contact, it is this continuous contact that a person using the string-along technic lacks. The person that is looking to string you along must be obvious as they will string you along or run drama on you in the times that you are not needed. This person will try small attempts to show you that you are needed in their life, typically only in an effort to try and make you feel bad. This is that drama that is involved when someone is running drama on you. One way that you can play their drama back on them is by running some game technics on this person.

Game strategies and technics will always trump drama technics. So when we're talking about running-game strategies and technics on a person, we would be looking to create a feeling within this person. This doesn't have to be a good or happy feeling as any feelings are good ones that can be used to control another person. Anger is actually one of the easiest feelings to play off of as creating feelings of anger are much easier to create than feelings of happiness. The overall goal of running game or drama is the same, and that is to gain control over you, your actions, and your money.

Some people are drawn to drama, believe it or not, to the point that they may miss the drama that a certain lifestyle may bring. Running drama would be like if someone was to tell you something that is untrue just to get a response out of you, as you can imagine there are lots and lots of things that a person could say to another person to get a response, but I'm going to give you a few examples.

A good example would be telling someone that you're going out to the club then actually just going to bed. Maybe a person may do things or say things to make you think you aren't the only one in their life. The examples can go on forever. The important thing to know is that when running drama, you are actually running lies, and it can be a telltale sign that someone is running drama on you when you find out that they are fabricating lies.

## Brand New

It is the strategy of the player to look to swoop on people that are brand-new to the type of games that people will play in the effort to control you in one way or another. The word *brand-new* refers to the person that isn't aware of the ulterior or interior motives for people doing the things they do. Typically it seems, if a person does or says something, your average person must think that their reasoning behind doing what they're doing is only obvious. However, people that are running drama or game will always have another reason for doing what they're doing as their motives may not seem so obviously clear, and this is what makes a person brand-new.

Once you have been around people that are running drama and or game, you will start to get used to the ulterior ways that people have. However, it is through this book that they must seem very obvious to you when you see them without ever having to go through all the hardship that comes with the knowledge that you will learn about here in this book. The fact that you are aware of these strategies will put you ahead of the game. The reason this book is so powerful is because game or the motives for running or playing games is done by people so that they can get the things they want out of people and life in general. So the strategies they used to do, this will be forever present, and when you least expect it, that's when you will find out that the game goes on and is always going to be.

## Planned Approach

You always want to have a planned approach no matter what situation you are in. This planned approach will help you to accomplish your goals in life. This planned approach can be used to run game as well. The reason a planned approach will be so helpful is because it will help you have an idea of what the beginning and the end result will look like. You want to approach most, all situations in life with the goal of gaining control so that you can be in control of your future. Well, this is very important when looking to use a planned approach when running game as your goal of the planned approach will be to gain control over a person as opposed to a situation.

However, you will need to provide the perfect situation for another person so that you may gain the control that you desire. One of the most important things you will need to remember is that you want to approach the person in a non-needy fashion. This is because any time you approach a person and you are needy for anything, you will be the one to be taken advantage of, as anybody that is aware of any type of game or that is a person that has any kind of common sense will see this and look to take advantage of a needy person.

If they don't look to take advantage of the situation, they will look to avoid it altogether.

Any time you are wanting something from someone else and they know about what you want, you will now have lost or given away the power that you originally have, as the power over you and the situation now sits in the other person's hands because you gave it away by letting the other person know in one way or another what it is you want from them. As whatever it is that you wanted, now becomes a bargaining chip of sort and will be used against you.

Remember, it is the goal of your planned approach to accomplish the task that you set out to accomplish. The goal that you wish to accomplish is gaining control over another person by providing them with their needs and the things that they want without them ever telling you what these wants and needs are so that we can play off of them making ourselves become the very thing that they need.

This is all done just so that we can get what it is that we want out of a person. As people are hesitant to ever want to provide another person with their needs, I ask the question *why would they?*

This is why game is so powerful, and power of any type is attractive to others, as you may hold a very powerful skill when you are able to provide people with their needs without them ever telling you what they are.

Your planned approach is very important and is not referring to approaching someone at all. But referring to what your overall goal will be in approaching them in the first place, in fact your plan of approach should be a fine strategy to get the other person to approach you, and when that don't work, you may want to try another direction and approach them directly. Your planned approach should let you know from the jump what you're wanting or needing, and your planned approach should be the blueprint to get it.

If your planned approach isn't working, then you failed to figure out what it is this person needs, and this will be why they aren't biting the bait that you threw out there. As everybody wants something, the word *wanting* itself shows that a person wants something because they don't have it. You want to be able to figure out what it is that this person wants so that you can provide it. There are a number of different avenues that you can choose to take as we have been talking about in this book in the other chapters.

One of the things I would advise against is thinking too much about what a person wants as you should be able to figure this out right away. If you find yourself thinking too much or too hard about what a person wants, it is my opinion that you can't figure out what they want because they don't know what they want themselves and thinking too hard about this will only draw you in closer to a position that you don't want to.

# Chapter 7

# Self

> I have learned this, it's not what one does that is wrong,
> but what one becomes as a consequence of it.
> —Oscar Wilde

THROUGHOUT THIS BOOK, WE HAVE been talking about game or basically knowledge of strategies and technics that can be used to gain the hearts and minds of others.

The reason we have been discussing this is because it adds to who you are as a person as it is a strength to be able to attract the thing that you desire in life. Well, throughout this chapter, we will be talking about self as it is from within yourself that you will find the answers to all your problems as this book is about game. Well, game starts from within who you are.

It's good to know exactly who you are and what you want and what you don't want. This way you can look to provide yourself with the things you want and desire out of life, eliminating the things that take time and energy away from gaining the things that you do want in your life.

One thing that I have learned to do is to talk to myself. I ask myself the questions that I want answers to. This is helpful because as people we tend to think that we know who we are, and we think that we know what we want. So I ask the question: "If you know who you are and you know what you want, then why are you doing things that bring about things that you don't want in your life, things that you really don't desire to be a part of? Why would you be doing things that don't openly show others that you are who you say you are?"

The reason this is so important is because this book you hold in your hands is about game and to have game is to have the ability to attract others to you. Once you are able to attract others to your intention will be the key to your success as your intention will be your end result or ultimate goal. And your ultimate goal is to get the things that you want in life, so it is very important to know who you are and what you want. If you don't know who you are and what you want, then you won't be able to figure out who other people are or what other people want either as this is very important when running game because to run game, you will be required to provide other people with the things they want.

So back to my question, "Who are you?" I suggest you ask yourself this question so that you may know the answer without question.

I asked the question, "What do you want?" And this is so that you can be working to gain the things that you want because so often people may find themselves working to gain something that they don't even really want. So it is my opinion that you should take the time to sit down with yourself and ask yourself, "What is it that I want? Or is this what I truly want for myself?" You may be surprised with the answer you get. If you can't figure out what it is that you really want, then I suggest you figure out what it is that you don't want as this may be very helpful in helping yourself figure out what you do want.

Once you have figured this out, then you may start to your character and personality, weeding out the qualities you don't want and adding in the qualities you do want. It's really that simple as you are you, and you are who you want to be, right? So then there's no reason you should ever find yourself not living up to be who you want to be. After all, you made you. It's not society or the things you've been through that made you who you are. You make you who you are. There's no reason that you shouldn't always be at the top of your game. You should always be the exact person that you want to be, and you should always do the things that that person would be doing.

For an example, if you do dumb shit, then you're gonna be a dumb shit. If you do scandalous things, then you're gonna be scandalous. If you do cool ass things, then you're gonna be cool.

If you do funny things, then you're gonna be funny, and these are the facts that have been proven to be true over and over. You must realize these things that we are talking about are based off of how you see or view you as other people will also see you as you see you as you being the person that you are and doing the things that make you you. This is another thing that will attract people to you, and that is the uniqueness that you carry within yourself as everyone is unique when they are being themselves. Of course, for you to be you, then you will need to know who you are.

If you don't like who you are or who you have become, then why don't you change this? If you can change your laugh, your smile, and the things that you laugh at, then why wouldn't you be able to change other things about yourself and just as you can change yourself if you aren't particularly happy about who you are? You can also change or add the necessary things that you need to in order to step your game up. This time that you have right now is your time slot here on earth, and when your time is up, then your time is up. You don't get any more time, so it is up to you to do what it is that you wish to do with it.

This is why I think it is so important to step your game up so that you may accomplish the goals that you wish to accomplish in life so you can be a better you and so that you can step it up on them in the effort for greatness within yourself.

There is an old saying and it goes like this: "If you knew better, then you would do better." This saying has to do with the end result of your actions as if you knew where these actions would lead you then you wouldn't be doing these things. Because they only lead to stress, dissatisfaction, heartache, and being broke. It is the person that knows better and still does the things that leads them to a bad situation that is really in trouble. This must seem obvious as to why I would say that because if you know the end result of a situation, there is no need for confirmation. And there is no need to have to prove something to yourself that you already know.

I ask the question, "If you can point out the bad or wrongful things that other people are doing as you may see exactly where their actions will lead them, then why can't you see these things within yourself and change them in the effort to step your game up?"

For example, if you are a loyal person, this is a good quality and trait, but if you're loyal to a person that is not loyal to you, then you can be looked at as foolish. If you agree with this, then you need to change this because if you don't, then you're no better than the person that knows better and still fails to do better. It's time to step it up on them, and by *them*, I mean everybody. The way that we do this is by stepping up who we are, leading the way for others to follow, and if they don't follow, then they are foolish.

## Brain Stimulation

Brain stimulation is another thing that draws people to you, and the reason it is so important to draw people to you is because that's what game is all about, getting people to be drawn to you. As when people are drawn to you, it is because they like you. So if you can't stimulate feelings within a person or if you're having trouble with your physical game, then you may choose the brain-stimulation route which would be considered part verbal and part mental game.

Stimulation being the keyword and stimulation can come in many forms, of course. Like we talked about, physical stimulation or stimulation of the eyes is the most important and most desired which is your physical game as people are attracted to things that are pretty or that look good as it stimulates the senses. Well, brain stimulation works like this: your goal is to stimulate the mind by basically providing new perspective and confirming some of the things that other people already know to be true and by teaching people the tools that are needed to step up their game up.

As everything in this book can be looked at as brain stimulation as people are attracted to learning, they like to be around people that can show them another way to view things and someone that teaches them things as they are drawn to the person that stimulates the brain naturally, as all people are drawn to people that can teach methods of survival within the atmosphere that another person lives in as this is a requirement of life and is actually apart of instinctual drives as people are driven to survive instinctually. And therefore, they are drawn to knowledge that will help them to do so. This knowledge stimulates the brain and sparks an interest within the person that is providing the knowledge and is a technic that can be called either gaming in or gaming down, depending on how you use this knowledge or how you present it as gaming in would be providing information or knowledge or game. It's all the same thing to another person for their own good. Like this book you hold in your hand can be considered a form of gaming in as this knowledge in this book was written for you to use in your own life for your advancement. However, the term gaming down is to say that I would be using this information as a form of brain stimulation to draw you in for my own advancement.

There are many instinctual drives that are imprinted on us as people for our own survival. These instincts are like a genetic code that cannot be altered and will never change. The number one thing that life requires is the need to survive. Without this need to survive, life and people would not exist. It is this need to survive that creates opportunity to be able to be the person that provides this for another person through knowledge as this knowledge or game will be the very thing that attracts people to you.

For an example, women have children, and so they are instinctually driven to provide for their children. So these instincts are imprinted within who they are, like how a dog is programmed to instinctually bark. It's just what they do. It comes natural as an instinct. Well, it is a natural instinct of a woman whether they have kids or not—to do what it is they have to do live better and to provide for their children once they have them. These are motherly instincts, so a woman is naturally attracted to a man that can provide this better life for their young and for themselves.

There may be many people that frown upon a woman that looks to be with a man that has a good job just because he has money. Well, it would be kinda silly if a woman was to be attracted to a man with no money and no job. Why would they do that? It makes no sense.

So this doesn't mean that a woman is a gold digger. This just means that she is smart and is only going with her maternal instincts to survive. Women are attracted to men that can provide instinctually, so if you're a man, then you better learn to provide. This is where game comes into play because this knowledge can feed a woman for life and is more like a lifelong-survival skill that gives a woman independence and frees her from the bondage that she is tied to instinctually to survive, and that is priceless to anybody.

This knowledge will be looked at as priceless information to both men and women as you must realize this information is life changing, and it is this information that will change your lifestyle and your outlook on life.

So I ask the question, "What is the price that can be placed on a new outlook on life? Again it is priceless and is not something that you can get from anybody. This is why this game is so valuable because it is life changing for both men and women, and it is very helpful to yourself and the game that you are running, all in an effort to draw people to you for your own self-betterment.

Playing on people's natural instincts is a great way to get people to be naturally drawn to you instinctually, just as men are naturally drawn in by women to have sex instinctually. It is hard for a man to go against his instincts and to tell a woman so unless she is unattractive. Well, this is also where having game comes into play. A man that considers himself to have game will say so because it is in his best interest as telling a woman so will only make them want you more. Please believe it's not like you're missing an opportunity. The man that has game in the effort to win over the girl and if the woman wants to have sex with you, then it is my opinion that you have already completed your mission. But at this point, the choice will be yours, and that is the whole point in having game.

Game is knowledge and to have this knowledge, you must understand where it comes from. All knowledge starts with the fear of God as this is where knowledge comes from. To understand where knowledge comes from, you have to understand where it is people came from as this knowledge you are looking to gain is knowledge of the world and how it works.

This knowledge is of the people in this world and how these people in this world work. The people in this world came from God as he is the one that gave us life. He is the one that gives us knowledge. So the beginning of any knowledge starts with the fear of God.

In the beginning of time, man was a lot like animals that had a daily goal to find food. That was all they did every day. The biggest goal of the day was to just find food.

So there would typically be two different ways to get the food. You would either hunt for it or you would gather berries. So you would either be a hunter or a gatherer. As time went on, the tools they used to hunt with started to get more and more advanced, and the materials that they used would start to become more vast in their tool making. As their tools would become more advanced, their jobs became easier. As their jobs got easier, their food supplies became greater and greater. As their hunting tools became more advanced, so did their farming equipment which created an overabundance of food.

This is when things really started to take off for man as there became more and more things to do besides look for food, and this is when people started branching out soon. There would be clothes makers and people that were skilled at building houses and so on. The reason I bring this up is because it is the tools that people had that were used to advance us as people. When our tools became more advanced, so did the people using them. So when we're looking for tools in modern times, these tools are found within the knowledge that we have as people of people. The more advanced our minds are in knowing how our minds work, the more we're able to work them to start to work for us.

So nowadays, there are many, many ways to get the things that we want, and the more there is to have, the more we want. The way we're going to get these things is by knowing how to work the people that have these things. As it seems anymore, everything is owned by somebody. You will need the skills needed to be able to draw these things away from someone. The way this is done is by making the people that have whatever it is we want to give it to us, and the way we make people want to do something is by offering them what it is they want or need. The trick to all of this is the knowledge of the things that people want that they aren't even aware that they want them. These things would be the things that we all desire in life without even knowing it.

For an example, everybody wants it all. There is no end to the things people desire in life. Everybody wants to be the man, and to be the man, you must have everything—the pretty girlfriend, a side girlfriend, many, many friends, and they want all the attention they can get. They want to make large amounts of money at every angle while doing the least, and they always want to appear smarter, bigger, and stronger than the next guy. They want the nice cars, and they want to be disloyal to their partner, but they want their partner to be loyal to them. These types of people have lost sight of the dream that they once had and have started to dream of the same things that everybody else has, although this may be okay.

The problem is that the goal is unrealistic, having everything and people get spread too thin. This is why you should have your own dream or goal that you intend to reach instead of having the same goals as others because it makes you weak in the same places as they are. The problem with people is within our wants. We always want what we don't have, so we lose sight of the true value of the things that we do have which took time and energy to gain and to keep. And now that we have them, we want something else. This is where game comes into play as it is our knowledge of this that puts us in the position to play off of these wants for our own betterment, and the key to our success will be found within our intention and what we intend to do with it.

One of the things that plagues us as people is boredom. As people get bored, they tend to do things that they wouldn't typically do. Another thing that people do is self-sabotage. When they're doing good and they're being successful, they will start to do things to sabotage this success. It is my opinion that this is done unknowingly as in they don't do it on purpose. I feel that it is done simply because a person's wants change. If we could keep our wants the same as they are and stop wanting new things as soon as we get the things that we want and to stop wanting so much, a person can become very successful when they have their own wants under control as you will always be able to find room for a hustle anytime there is change or fluctuation. This change and fluctuation can be found in our wants and needs as they may change or fluctuate.

This means that a person leaves themselves open to be hustled or taken advantage of when their wants change or fluctuate. This is why it is so important to get your wants under control and you understand the importance of not wanting too much because, as a person, it makes you weak and needy.

## Time

We are all strapped for our time as we are only allotted so much time in this world. What you do with your time is up to you. I recently read a study that said the average person lives 25,555 days in their life. This means we are under a time restraint which only gives us a certain amount of time to accomplish our goals. So the question becomes, "What will you do with your 25,555 days?" Where a person chooses to spend their time is typically going to be a big indicator as to what they're interested in.

If a person spends a lot of time playing golf, you could say that person is interested in golf because they spend so much time entertaining the game and the idea of golf. If a person spends a lot of time involving themselves in politics, then you could say this person is interested in entertaining the idea of politics. It gets to the point that the game of golf or the talk of politics is actually being entertained by the person interested in them instead of the other way around. The same goes for people when someone is interested in you, they will spend their time with you or want to spend their time with you.

They may talk about you when you're not around thinking and entertaining the idea of you. Well, what this does is it gives a person something to do. It gives them entertainment as they are the ones actually being entertained by you.

When you may be nowhere to be found, the problem is that people are left entertaining people that aren't even present or games that they play and/or are interested in which is really just a distraction to people and to what their real goals may be which keeps people from accomplishing their goals and becoming successful at achieving their dreams as they're left dreaming about games of golf and politics.

It is my opinion that instead of entertaining other people and games that they like to play that we should be looking to gain knowledge. Knowledge of how the things we are interested work so that we can work them instead of just entertaining the idea. So through this next chapter, we will be talking about how people work so that we may know how to work them to our full advantage. It has always been my opinion that as people we should be looking for ways to build each other up instead of tearing each other down.

However, most people are too worried and not ever truly loyal enough to make this happen.

So if you find it just as difficult as I have to find people that are looking to build each other up, then you may have better luck working them to your advantage through knowing just how they work, as this is exactly how other people attempt to do toward you as they always seem to try to take an advantage of others.

However, taking advantage of others will not be our goal. Our goal will be to take advantage of those that try to take advantage of us. This is typically an easy thing to do as whenever you know what a person wants, you will know how to work them to your advantage. Depending on what a person wants will be the deciding factor in whether or not they are looking to take an advantage of you or if they are only looking to just take advantage of the things that you have to offer.

These two sound the same, but they are very different as all people are looking to take an advantage of the things you have to offer. But some people are straight out only looking to take an advantage of you in the coldest way.

These are the people that you want to avoid at all costs because these are the people that really have little to nothing to offer you. They just want to take from you and leave you in the dust with nothing. These are the people that never had any interests in you in the first place.

Their only goal was to take from you for their own advancement, although it is my opinion that everybody is only in it for their own advancement.

However, you want to stay away from those that have nothing to offer you so that you may advance off of them in some way or another. Do not get confused as every person is looking to take advantage of all the things you have to offer such as your smile, your jokes, your sex, your money.

The list goes on forever. It is very common for one to wonder what it is that a person wants from another person. Well, it is my opinion that they want to take an advantage of all the things you have to offer. The difference between the person that is like most people that look to take advantage of all you have to offer and the person that only looks to take advantage of you for one particular thing is that they are only using you to get what they want. Although it might sound backward, I assure you it's not.

For an example, when a person meets another person, we'll say when a woman meets a man that she likes, you may hear her say, "He's so charming, and he has a good job. He's a handsome man with no kids, and his sex is spectacular." This would be your typical person that is only looking to take an advantage of all that you have to offer, basically saying that she likes the whole package of everything you offer.

Now the person that is only looking to take an advantage of you for your sex, money, or good times that you have to offer won't typically be talking about you at all, but if they do, they would only be bringing up the one thing that you do have to offer just to make themselves look like they're on top of their game by using you to their advantage. The person that only wants one thing from you whether it be sex, money, or anything else will be the person that is using you.

It can sometimes be hard to come to grips with the reality of the situation. Women use men, and men use women. Just be aware of the person that is only looking to use you for one thing in particular. However, it will be the person that gives away what it is that they are using you for that will put themselves in the position to be taken for a ride as you may now use this item as a sort of bargaining chip.

However, like I said, I would advise against doing so because it puts you in the position where people are wanting something today for an exchange for something in the future which puts you in the position to be hustled.

There are all kinds of hustles out there, and running game is one of the more prominent or successful. It's so successful because it deals with gaining the hearts and minds of those around us. Once you have done that, anything is possible. However, many people seem to be confused on the difference between running game and playing games with each other for their own advancement. This is very important as you will be able to run your game around those that are only playing games instead of running game, allowing those that are playing games to be sucked in by the powerful game that you are running. The reason people that are playing games as opposed to those that are running game are not as successful is because nobody is drawn to someone that is playing games like they are to someone that is running game.

One of the big differences in people running game and the people playing games is that the person playing games is only playing themselves. As they attempt to draw you in for their own self-betterment, the games that they are playing must seem lame and obvious. Their intentions in playing games are poor and of the self-loathing nature that only bring about a negative end result for their actions. And this is exactly why the games they play are unsuccessful because their goal is almost nonexistent or is one of poor nature. This is exactly why it is good to be aware of the strategies and technics that are a part of having game so that you can easily point out those that are playing games.

People are drawn to people that have game because it is a skill that will help build people up in their lives while people that are only playing games drag people down for their own self-advancement. So like I promised, this next chapter is about how people work and how to work them.

We work them by playing their little game to our advantage which would make you better at their own game than they are. And that's how we will be getting up under their skin which creates thoughts which bring about emotions that bring about feelings. As always, once you have created feelings within that person, then you have won.

People will attempt to play many games in the effort to see if you will play them as they tend to feel as if them getting you to do what they want is a way for them to show their power over you as it must seem obvious if a person is able to tell you to do something and you do it. It makes them feel as if they have control over you as this person may tell you to leave their house then try to get you to come back, and they may be very rude to you before you leave as this is just another way for them to show their power over you. These games do not draw people. In fact, it actually pushes them away.

This person may even tell you after you leave their house that they never wanted you to leave when you know that they definitely did want you to leave. This is a running-drama technic that is based upon lies. These lies are used by people to try and get you to feel a certain way.

The one thing that these games do is create emotions and feelings of anger. As we learned earlier in the book, anger is one of the easiest feelings to play off of. Do not let these people playing games with you get you to the point that they're able to create feelings of any kind within you.

People will sometimes try the subliminal-message technic on you. Typically, this is just another way to get you to feel a certain way which is just another technic used by people to try and create feelings inside of you so that they can get you to act a specific way. The subliminal-message technic works like this: a person will play off of music on the radio or maybe talk about another person, saying negative things about this other person when really they're talking about you. Again, they do this so that they can create feelings of inadequacy within you. Again, the number one thing you want to avoid is allowing yourself to catch any type of feelings.

At this point, you must be asking yourself **_why would I ever want to be involved with a person that is trying to treat me in such a manner?_** Well, you don't or shouldn't want to, but the fact of the matter is that you need to be able to recognize this behavior from the jump as this type of behavior is actually counterproductive for the person trying to play these games. As this person is attempting to create feelings inside of you, they will actually be just creating feelings inside themselves, if you don't play along.

There are many games people will play, and my story about how a person may call you over to their house then do things to make you leave is just an example of one as the idea behind the story is what's important. And what's important is how people will try and play you like a puppet if you let them, as people do what you let them do, and the fact of the matter is that they wouldn't do it if you didn't let them.

So you must be aware that people will look to test their boundaries to see what you will let them get away with. When they do, it is important to let them know right away that you are not putting up with any bs that they're trying to throw your way.

Do not attempt to play dumb because you feel that you are getting what you want out of the relationship because it just leads to disrespect. It will also cause people to act as if the thing they have done wrong to you never happened. This is all part of running drama, laying games. It's all the same, and it is done by others so they can feel as if they're playing you when really they're just playing themselves. However, these games are run by people that are looking to attempt to produce feelings inside of someone, much like the backward game as the backward game is a game that people like to play in the effort to create feelings inside of you. As anytime you can make a person emotional, it will start to create feelings, and feelings of any kind are still feelings.

The backward game is when you tell a person that they are doing all the things that you are actually doing. Again, this is done to create feelings of anger inside someone, and as we know, feelings of any kind are still feelings.

I do not recommend that you play any of these games. I'm only pointing them out so that you know about them, and you do not allow yourself to play into them as this is exactly how you will find yourself to be successful in not allowing yourself to play into the games that other people create just to create feelings inside of you.

## The Game of Life

The biggest game of all is the game of life, and this is the most important game of all. One of the reasons you don't want to start playing games with people is because you don't want your life to become a game. Running game is a skill, and this skill can be used to help you win in the game we call life. Whether you win or lose the game of life will be based upon what you consider winning. I'm not sure anyone can tell you how to win the game of life, but I do know that you must have balance in your life in your activities and within your mind.

This balance is what everyone must have in their life if one wants to have their life feel complete. It is this balance that you will be able to play off of, as a person that may have a good and happy home life with their significant other may be missing that excitement that a moment of single living may bring. They may be missing feelings of really truly being desired by another person. The person that has many, many partners may be missing the solidarity that a quality, loving relationship may bring. The person that has lots of money may be missing the feelings of acceptance of others.

Before you decide to play off of the missing piece in someone else's life, I suggest that you look to find some balance in your life. This balance is mainly within your mind and body, balancing your thoughts and desires that are desired by or for the mind. This would include your feelings of any type as your thoughts are what bring about feelings. Your body will crave things much like the mind. However, the body is much less complicated as the body wants to feel companionship and warmth from another person. The mind may tell you that it wants this from a specific person although this other person may be poisonous to the mind and the body. You will need to find a balance of acceptance within someone that is not hazardous to either.

If you don't, you may find yourself being the one that is taken advantage of in your moment of lost balance.

Some people try to balance the partners in their life as there may be many. However, this paralells people that are playing games as opposed to someone that is running game.

The balance in your own life is the thing that you want to focus on, making sure that you have a perfect balance of all things. This is so that you won't be found wanting or needing much from another person. One of the things that everybody does need from another person is sex and love. Do not get these two mixed up as they are definitely different. Love feeds the mind and desires of the heart while sex is something that you can get anywhere. However, you should be looking to get both of these in the same place. You will need to keep a healthy mind to keep the affection of another person as all things are conditional and come with conditions, even love. For example, if you were to go out and violate the terms in which this love is bound by such as loyalty, you might just find out how conditional love can be. It is my opinion that unconditional love is the sickest type of love as it comes with no conditions. Meaning, no matter what happens, the other person will still love the other which creates an atmosphere that is poisonous to the mind. After you are able to find a healthy balance of things to feed the body and mind, you can now start to play off of the lack of balance in other's lives, figuring out exactly what another person may be lacking in their life to balance it out for them, if and when it is in your benefit.

The very reason that we run game is so that we can advance and grow and win in the biggest game of all the game of life. To do so, we will need to stay forever changing as anything that is growing will be changing.

The more you are changing, the more that you are growing, and the overall goal is to be the best that you can possibly be. This means that you will need to be forever looking to step your game up in every way.

One of the ways that you can be sure to do this is by working on your three parts of the game. Your physical which is your looks, your body, and your hygiene, these are the things that are required of you to be sure that you are up on your physical game. Your mental game is your knowledge of how other people work, knowing what they want and what they desire so that you can use it against them by making yourself the person that can provide these needs for your own advancement. Your verbal game is based upon being able to talk to people and to be able to say the right types of things to draw a person in, such as knowing what a person is interested in and using the center strategy which is knowing who a person is based off of their center.

If you want to win in life, it is my opinion that the only way to do so is through working on who you are as a person and making sure that you have gained the hearts and minds of those around you so that you can use them to your advantage and so that you can stay advancing in life.

The game of life is much like driving a car, and of course, you want to be driving the nicest car possible. This would be a representation of your physical game, keeping up on your physical game so you may have the best-looking person as you can possibly be. One of the most important things in driving a car is your destination as this destination will be a representation of your intentions or your ultimate goal and end result in which you intend to reach.

Now you want to make sure that you're driving in the right direction because if you're not, you might just find yourself driving in circles which many people do.

This is why your intention is so important because if you don't have a destination, then driving around aimlessly might be looked at as if you're driving around for fun. But being lost is no fun, it is more or less an excuse for failure as you may be accepting of ending up wherever you do end up. As at this point, you will have no choice but to accept where do end up. You want to make sure that while driving, you try to not have any accidents or cause any wrecks. If you do, you will definitely want to have insurance. This insurance can be looked at as having a backup plan of some sorts. This backup plan may be a set of people that got your back so that, driving or not, you stay traveling smoothly down the road of life.

A car is made up of various parts that when they all come together, it creates a fine vehicle capable of traveling anywhere, and since this car is a representation of you, you'll want to make sure that you stay versatile and capable of anything. It is important that you have a good-skill level accompanied with the right qualities and traits so that when they all come together, it creates a machine that is well oiled and ready to drive smoothly.

Much like a car is when it has all its parts and is operating correctly, you will need to choose a route to take to get to your destination which is a representation of you knowing which roads or avenues to take to get to your destination.

Not everybody chooses to take main streets as some like to take back roads, trying to avoid doing the things required by society to get to their destination. While others obviously prefer the freeway whenever possible as they seem to be speeding through life. Some people seem to always be driving on cruise control, just coasting through life not really having any ups and downs, highs or lows, just one smooth trip as it seems they prefer which is okay, but it keeps you from advancing in any large amounts at one time in a single trip. How you prefer to drive is up to you. Will you be an angry driver that is constantly road raging, middle finger in the air blaming everyone around you for you being late to make it to your destination? Will you drive your car too hard until it breaks down and is on the side of the road? Will you be a driver that ignores all the many signs as you drive down this road, signs like top or dead end or maybe signs that say, "Please don't drink and drive"? Will you be a driver that stays in your lane or maybe the driver that rides the shoulder lane getting over at the las-t minute. One thing is for sure, much like in driving an actual car, any time you look to take shortcuts, it seems that every time you only end up getting lost trying to do so. There are no shortcuts in nature, and just like how nature takes its course, so does life, and it is my opinion that anytime you are looking for a shortcut in life that you will find that this shortcut will either have you lost or this shortcut will actually be a lot longer road to travel when driving down the road of life.

So when you are driving down the road of life, you're going to need to know which roads are dead ends. You will need to be able to read the signs as these signs are typically signs of things to come. This is why having game is so valuable because it will allow you to be able to read the signs that people are putting out there for you to see. This will help you to make wiser decisions about where, in which way you will want to let people into your life as everybody has a value and a use. Your game will draw them to you then all you must do is assign them a value and a position along with a role to play in your life as we continue to stay stepping our game up to the next level, staying ahead of the competition.

As the game of life goes on, there will be many games others will attempt to play on you. It is the games that we play on ourselves that need to be addressed and regulated. As the game goes on, it is your game or knowledge of game and the strategies and technics that we develop to work in our favor that will take us places as our game is the thing that attracts others to us. If you want to attract, then you must be attractive, and as we know, there are many ways to attract the things that we want as there is many ways to be attractive. People will always be attracted to you for one reason or another. The trick is to get them to be attracted to you for the correct reasons.

It is through maximizing the amount of different possibilities for another person from within yourself and who you are that will draw people to you. However, these people are definitely drawn to you for a selfish reason as most all people are. It is the person that has game that can recognize this selfishness in others and use it to their advantage as most people are so selfish and blinded by it to the point that they harm themselves with their selfish ways. This is why it is a powerful tool and a cunning way to advance by providing others with their needs so that you may get what you want from the person without them ever expecting a thing.

## Kings and Queens

Even kings and queens have to treat their people in their kingdom good as it is the people in the kingdom that make up their kingdom. If it wasn't for the people, then the kings and queens wouldn't have anybody or anything to rule over. So who's more important, is it the kings and queens or the people they rule over? It seems that the people are just as important as the kings and queens that govern over them. This is why it is important for you to be aware of how important the people around you really are as it is these people that make you who you are, and it is these people that will help you build your kingdom.

It is the people around you that allow you to be the person that you are because if it wasn't for the people around you being who they are, then you couldn't be who you are. The same goes for kings and queens. If the king was to treat his people poorly, the people will rise up against him and look to overthrow the king and appoint a new one, a king that will treat his people fairly so that the people of the kingdom may have a chance at being happy and successful as well. If you look at things for what they really are, it seems the people actually have more power than the king. This is why the king must not be too selfish to remember just why he is king.

## The Reward System

Every person in the whole world works off of the same system, and that system is the reward system. Although sometimes people may do things out of the kindness of their heart, that's temporary as nobody in this world can afford to just go around all day like Santa Claus doing good deeds out of the kindness of their own heart. Everyone must find ways to get money, so they can live. Most people get jobs to pay their bills. When they go to these jobs, there is an understanding between the employer and the employee. The employer understands that you're going to work a certain amount of hours for a certain amount of money.

If you don't work the hours, then you don't get paid the money, and that's how the reward system works. This system is seen in every aspect of life as anytime someone does something for another person, they expect a reward of sorts. It has gotten to the point that people will actually offer to do something for another person in the hopes of a reward when the other person isn't even aware that the other person even wants a reward. People do this all the time, and if you don't want to give up the reward, there may be repercussions as it is common for this person to say that you owe them even when there was never an understanding of a reward.

This reward system is a tool that you can use to your advantage. By working on yourself and who you are and what you have to offer, you can make your presents be the reward as a person that isn't up on their game or aware of how they appear to others isn't going to be much of a reward to be around. Anytime there is a system with a set of rules and/or principles, there will be a way to take an advantage of the system and a way to manipulate it to your liking.

The reward system is no different, and by taking the proper steps to make your presents the reward, you may take an advantage of this system. As many people will do many things in the effort to work toward gaining your presents, you may look at it as your presents is their presents or their reward for their actions. However, you must remember how the reward system works. When you do what's expected of you, then you get the reward. When you don't do what is expected, then you get no reward, and you must play this system just as it's designed to work or it won't work.

This is exactly why you want to work on yourself and the things that your presents has to offer to somebody else as the reward system only works if the other person is interested in the reward that is offered.

## The More Plentiful

The more plentiful something is, the lesser the value. This is not an opinion but a fact. This can best be seen in our own economy as things become more plentiful such as some of our precious metals may have a high price on them until the metal becomes more plentiful. At the point these metals are more plentiful, the price goes down and is a direct reflection on the fluctuating metal prices. Much like fruit in the wintertime, the prices go up, and in **the** summertime, they go down. This is because in the summertime, fruit is everywhere, and it is more plentiful and so it's cheaper.

The same set of principles apply for people as well, as there may be many people that are all the same.

They have no drive and no real goals of any kind and are typically too selfish to see the different possibilities that are possible. This means that you may drive your own value that you carry by making yourself unique. This doesn't mean that you should try to be different from everybody else. This means that you can be different than everybody else by driving the value that you carry by stepping your game up which will make you unique as many people aren't game savvy and, for lack of a better word, with the shit.

There are many things that you can do to make yourself be set aside from the rest. By basically stepping your game up and becoming game tight and working on your three parts of the game, your physical, mental, and your verbal now, of course, there are many things besides those three parts of game that will make you a set aside from the rest-type person. Those are also in this book, and those would be figured out on a person-by-person basis. This is why you're better off working on your three parts of the game. However, the idea is to become more valuable by becoming a set-aside individual by allowing others to see the uniqueness that you hold over others. Sometimes this can be done by having a higher calling or a mission to complete as it makes you different than others because most do not.

A person that is loyal is also something that is not that common, so it makes a person more valuable as a person that has loyalty is not so plentiful so their value goes up. Just as a person that has any real, true game is not that common, so it makes them more valuable. These are traits and skills that you can add or subtract from who you are in the effort to drive your value up from within who you are and how others will assess you as your value will be assessed. The same goes for disloyalty as a person that is disloyal may be seen to have no value. However, as long as the person isn't disloyal to you, even if they are to others, you may find some value in their disloyalty to others, although disloyalty is very common and is not going to drive anyone's value up because disloyalty is a trait that is all to plentiful in people.

## Be a Winner

It doesn't matter what the situation may be. Every time in every situation, you want to be a winner. You want to win and come out on top every time, and this is done by creating a goal then a personalized set of steps that will get you to your goal as long as you follow the steps necessary to accomplish the goal. You will reach your goal.

You should never question why you are doing something because you should already know why you're doing what you're doing. And you should be following the steps in your personalized goal so that you can be accomplished in life and in your personal goals.

The only time you should be questioning yourself and the things that you're doing is when you find yourself losing. This is so that you can rethink your strategies and technics along with your personalized set of steps that have been set forth for you to achieve your goal. Then you may approach the situation differently so that, in the end, you will come out winning. If you're not winning, then you're losing, and you can't do both win and lose at the same time. So you will need to pick one. You choose to be the winner or the loser. In every situation, the choice will be yours, and this is why you want to look to put yourself in win-win situations as these win-win situations will help you to be successful in accomplishing your goals and to be a winner.

When you put yourself in a win-win situation, there is no losing. You can position yourself in this type of position by not entering any situation that does not benefit you in some sort of way. It also helps if you are to look at every situation as a possible opportunity as every problem you face is a possible opportunity as long as you can see the opportunity among the problem. There is always room for you to advance in a positive or a negative situation. However, it is up to you to find a way to make this happen.

No matter what the situation, you must keep the option open to cut your losses, not hanging on to the unbeneficial as you may always be able to cut your losses at any point which would mean that you will no longer be losing and that you will now be winning as you are now back on the winning path. This is a good way to keep yourself in a win-win situation as many people get to the point that they feel they have too much invested in someone or something that they can't just cut their losses. However, this way of thinking just keeps you on that losing path that leads to nowhere. You must always keep the option to cut your losses and bail as sometimes it is necessary, and keeping this option open is a great way to put yourself in that win-win situation.

## Losses and Gains

As in all games, the object of the game is to win. The last thing you want to do is lose. And you stay winning by making sure that you are gaining from each and every relationship. This is the idea behind having game so that you may stay advancing off of all your relationships. This should be a common factor in both people playing the games and people running game. It is a sign of someone playing games and attempting to use you when a person overreacts and gets mad over taking a small loss. This is because that they entered the situation with the thought of taking money and other tangible gains from you. When they end up taking a loss, they will tend to get mad even over the smallest loss.

This is the difference in people playing games and people that have game. The person that has game would never get mad over a small loss as it should be looked at as an investment in gaining the heart and mind as you will always gain more out of a long-term relationship than you will from a short one. Do not focus on small gains to the point that you lose the hearts and minds of others as it is counterproductive to your game. And always be aware of the person that overreacts over small loses as it is a sure sign of someone feeling as if you got one up on them instead of them getting one up on you.

Another thing someone that is playing games will attempt to do is to point you out to be doing things that you're not doing. These things may be terrible things, things that you might not ever think of doing. They do this to create feelings of anger inside of you. They also do this to help make themselves feel better about the things that they have been doing toward you as this person may feel as if they have an excuse for doing the things that they have been doing. This strategy parallels the backward game.

## Saying No

Saying no to people is another thing that draws people to you. This is because it creates a boundary, letting people know that you're not a sucker, and you're not just going to say yes to anything and everything. People are drawn to people that say no to them because it causes them to think that you're not needy. It also shows that you don't particularly need something or want something from them. This is what causes people to work hard to get you on their team and to start saying yes to them because people want things that they can't have or don't have. Saying no to people can be a lot harder than it sounds to some, but I assure you saying no is an awesome strategy that can be used to draw people in. It may save you more times than not and will help to draw people in.

## Interior and Exterior

There are two types of problems people face, and these are interior and exterior. This means that all the problems we face will be from the interior which is from the inside of the body or from the outside of the body which is the exterior. Now I used the word *problems* because the word *problems* describe what comes after we want or need something. It becomes a problem when we want something or we don't have something. So every problem we face will be an interior or an exterior problem, and it is important for you to know which is which so that you don't find yourself trying to fix an exterior problem with an interior source.

As there are many things that we need as people and to secure your wants and needs, you will need to fulfill both your interior and exterior needs. This is so that you won't be found wanting. Another reason that you want to secure both your interior and exterior needs is so that you can start providing others with their needs. And of course, this is only so that you can draw people in as people are drawn to fulfilling their own needs, and you want them to see that you are the solution to their needs which is a problem for them but an opportunity for you.

## The Unknown

People fear the unknown, and it is this fear that we will feed on as the mystery is always greater than the reality, and it is this mystery that we will create in the effort to draw people in. This mystery is created by saying no to people and by always being on the go as this causes people to wonder why you won't talk to them. What do you do in your spare time? And what exactly makes you tick along with what you're interested in? Sometimes this also causes people to wonder why you don't seem so interested in them when everybody else is.

The goal behind feeding on fear is to cause confusion as people are puzzled by what they don't understand. Of course, people don't understand the things that they are puzzled about, and so it creates this magnetic-type-like atmosphere where people that are confused or are left in the dark to think about the things they don't understand are drawn to you. As the mystery about you draws them in, the more and more they think about you. So anytime you can create confusion or mystery, people will be drawn to you as this confusion and mystery makes you attractive to those that don't understand why it is you are doing what you're doing or if they don't have a clue as to what you're doing or what you're really about.

So it's good to let people wonder about you because when people start to feel as if they know who you are and exactly what you're about, they will find a way to use you to their advantage as they start to get comfortable with you. One of the last things you want is for someone to get comfortable because when people get too comfortable, they start to be themselves. The more they start to be themselves, the more they start to think about themselves. The more they think about themselves, the less they think about you. You definitely want them to have their thoughts on you, not themselves.

It is a good strategy to keep someone's thoughts so mixed up by thinking about you and what you're doing that they barely have time to think about themselves, causing confusion to the point that they are left to think up conclusions about you which causes stress on the mind and body. This stress is what creates emotions when accompanied with uncontrollable thoughts of what could be. These thoughts of constant confusion are addicting as they give people something to do as so many people have become bored with their lives and really don't have many things that are to interesting to do throughout their day, and the things that they do are all the same things, day in and day out, so it is this mystery that creates excitement, and all people must have something exciting going on in their lives to make it a life worth living.

When you are looking to game someone in, there is no need for you to wait for someone to tell you what it is they need in their life. What they need is someone that can be the person that everybody else is not. As most, all people are looking to gain in some way or somehow off of the relationship they desire from you, the goal is to be the person that others aren't as most people are lame, for lack of a better word, and aren't capable of providing themselves with their own needs, so they definitely aren't going to be able to provide you with your needs.

You can make yourself different from others by providing a new way to look at things as providing a new perspective for someone and a new way to look at things will make you appear as if you are different than others. As the things you say are different and the way you make them feel is different which will make you different, different is good when there is so much of the same thing out there, and you want to make yourself appear set aside from the rest. It is good to have good reasoning behind the things that you say to people as when you have good reasoning to back up your thoughts. You may be able to convince anybody of anything.

It also helps if the things that you are talking about are things that people care about. Touching on some of the more prominent issues that we are faced with as people as you do so you want to make yourself appear as if you may be the solution to their problem as you should be looking to gain the trust of another person when you are talking to them. However, do not use the words *you can trust me*, as these words should always be a red flag, letting you know that this person is trying to gain your trust intentionally. When someone is looking to gain your trust intentionally, it is typically because they have an ulterior motive for doing so.

However, relationships are built on trust. All relationships of any kind will be built on trust. So by making yourself appear loyal to another person, maybe in a past situation or maybe just loyal to being a specific way of thinking, making yourself appear loyal is achieved by being real in the things that you talk about. You can make yourself appear real in the things you say by talking about real things that matter to people. Another great part of being real in the things that you are talking about is the ability to see the other side of things in real-life scenarios as this is typically a good way to be able to create a funny moment in which someone may get lost in the moment with you.

Even if just for a moment, anytime you can take someone away for just a second and show them another way of thinking and a new perspective on how they see things they will be drawn to you.

# Chapter 8

# Play the Role

> In the game things are always subject to change,
> must be sure your direction stays the same.
> —Auzanae Barnett

EVERYBODY HAS A ROLE THAT they must play in life, and it is this role that makes them who they are. It is up to you to decide who you will be, and you will pick your role through your actions in the things that you choose to do daily, as it will be all the little things that you do.

That will add up to making you, you which is who you are. Much like at any job or business, there will be many people that have a specific job or duty in which they are supposed to carry out. Typically, there will be one's boss that may be called a supervisor, and the supervisor's job is to watch over the employees.

Then there is the supervisor's boss which may be the manager, and the manager has a boss and so on. The point is that everybody has a job or a role that they must play, and these roles come with certain lifestyles. Some lifestyles may be harsher than others, depending on which role you play. Although it's not so easy to just decide that you're going to play the role of the boss or supervisor, when it comes to life, you do get to just pick your role and then play your role well. You get to do this because it is your life, and since it's your life, it's your show. Since it's your show, you get to pick the role. So which role will you play? Will you be the strong, silent type of person that is not outgoing? Will you be the pushover that gets taken an advantage of left and right? Will you be the homeless guy on the side of the freeway asking for change outside the corner stores?

Will you be the guy that gives the homeless guy some change? Will you be a big spender or the person that is a tight wad with their money? The choice is yours, and although sometimes it may seem as if you're not in the position to make the choice, when really you're the only person that does get to make the choice. Nobody can or will make this choice for you and using the excuse that you're doing what you can with what you got is just a cop-out, an excuse for not trying, and the truth is by not picking a role, you are still picking a role in life just not a role in your own life.

Just as everyone that is in your life will have a role as well whether they pick this role or they are given this role by you as sometimes people that just want to be in your life will be happy to play any role given to them.

However, it is up to you to pick the role that you will play in life, and you want it to be a role that will put you in the position to where others will allow you to assign them a role in your life. As you can pick your role or character that you choose to be in life, you can do this by setting a set of standards that you hold yourself up to as well as others around you by acting a specific way and carrying yourself a certain way and having a certain air about yourself that will attract others to you. Having game will help you to attract others to you but to carry yourself in a certain way so that people are attracted to you is typically referred to as swag. Your swag is your style, the way you carry yourself and how you act on a regular. It is the air about you that attracts someone to you from the moment they meet you. And it is this swag that will be one of the deciding factors when it comes to determining which role that you will be playing in life.

This is why game is so important because it puts you in the position to where you will have a better role in life. One that has lots of benefits and puts you into the position where anything is possible. If you were in a room full of people, no matter where you're at if you take a moment to look around the room at the people in it, you will see the different roles that people play clearly based upon what they're doing and what types of things they do regularly.

Your girlfriend or boyfriend has a role. Our mom has a role. Our brothers and sisters have a role. And just as they have a role, you too have a role that you must play so that you can be who you are. Now any one person may be playing many roles for each and every social setting. And it is my opinion that the person that does so is attempting to fit in with that social set of people and is typically the person that doesn't know who they are yet.

You want to play the same role in every setting that you are in, never changing up so that you can fit in.

This is because you want others to be trying to fit in your life in any role that they can as you play the role of the big dawg or the role of the man or the woman or the boss or maybe the player. As we discussed, there are many roles, and you want your role to be a good one so that you may start picking out others and assigning them a role to play as well. When you do assign others a role in your life, you want to make sure that they are aware of their role and that they play it well because if they don't, someone else will. As knowing your role is like knowing your place and just as you want others in your life to know their role and to play it well, you should hold yourself up to knowing your role and playing it just as well. When you think about it, life is like a big game, and we're all just part of the game, and we must know our moves and our roles and play them well as every person in your life should have their purpose. And if they don't serve their purpose, then maybe they're serving their own purpose. It is up to you to decide who serves what purpose is best in your life so that you can organize these people in the correct manner. For the betterment of your own life and for your purpose, for example, someone may be a good friend to you, but they may be a terrible mother or father. Or they may be a good mother or father, but they may be a bad business partner. By organizing these people in your life and assigning them a role along with a value, you will be much more successful in running game and life itself.

You may look at these people as members of your team, and it is up to you to pick a winning team. As in any winning team, every member on the team must serve their purpose and play their role on the team. Each team member is going to be on the team for their own reasons or benefits, like always, and to keep these people on the team, you will need to provide them with something that they need so they must provide you with your needs or for whatever you desire to have them on your team for. It is best if the members on your team aren't aware of all the members that you have on the team so that you may use their strengths individually or combined. The choice is yours.

The members of your team will need to be trustworthy, and they must trust you as well as it is this trust that will be the glue that bonds you together.

It is important that you keep the members on your team to a limit as not everybody will qualify. Although everybody will have a use, it doesn't mean that they need to be considered a member of your team. The members on your team must trust the fact that you will always have their best interest in mind if you want them to do the same.

Your first string or closest team members should be close to being considered equals as they should be on the team for the same reason that you are for trust and unity. It is very important for you to show appreciation to the members on your team as it is much easier to give people praise than things that are worth a physical value, as praise has a value as well, and it doesn't cost you anything to give praise to another. People have the tendency to rise to the occasion and thrive when in a positive environment. And it will be up to you to provide this environment as it is this environment that can be used to draw them in.

It is important that you never show disloyalty to another member of your team right in front of another member because it proves disloyalty, and it will push people away. The whole reason in having a team is because the team makes your life better. So a good rule of thumb is if they make your life better, then you need them. But if they make your life worse, then you don't need them on your team or in your life.

As long as you continue to operate in this manner, then you will prosper in life. As people, we are always growing, and it will be the decisions that you make that will point you in the direction that may be a successful one or not, depending on your decision making. The idea behind having a team of people on your side is that when you have the hearts and minds of those around you, you will be successful as opposed to those that don't have the hearts and minds of those in their immediate circle.

The key to your success will be your judge of character so that you may build a good team. This is a good strategy to use in life, and it is also a hustle as a good hustler knows that. A hustle is when you enter a situation with another person to make a deal of sorts. When the deal or arrangement is set and is considered a done deal and both of you walk away from the deal, although the other person feels as if they have made a good deal or arrangement, you yourself is the one that came out on top, leaving the other person to think that they got what they wanted. So they are happy, and they got worked over.

So building a team can be looked at as a hustle as you want to be sure to be the person advancing the most off of any relationship you may have. However, the goal is to make the other person happy with the current situation.

As anytime you do business with someone, you want the end result in them doing business with you is also to make them happy.

## Playing Cards

Let's say your life is like a game of cards, and as in all games, we play them to win. Though sometimes it seems as if we have been dealt a terrible hand and we may be left feeling like it may be impossible to win, if you allow yourself to feel this way, then you have already lost as you have already defeated yourself in your own head.

You must not beat yourself down as others are already trying to do that for you on a daily basis.

As you look at your handful of cards, you will be thinking of your next move. Although you may have a shitty hand of cards, you can be sure that the way you play these cards is of an utmost importance to you winning the game. These cards in your hand should be looked at as your options, and you want to play the cards that open up more options for you as these options give you the power of choice, and these options put you in control of your future. No matter where you're at in life, you always want to look to open up options.

These options are brought about through having a high-skill level. No matter what cards you have in your hand, you can be sure to play them to your advantage when you have the skills to do so. These skills are brought about through education and practice, perfect practice to be exact.

You want to learn this game inside and out, and you will want to know everything there is to know about this game.

This is so that you can become the best player possible; however, the game that we are all playing is the game of life.

And in this game of life, our cards get replaced by people as it is these people that are going to give us what we want.

So these people are going to be looked at as our options and much like cards. These people come with different moves and possibilities.

Whether if you win or not will also be determined by your desire to win. By reading this book, it seems obvious to me that you are heading in the right direction, and that your desire to win is high. And you want to give yourself a chance at winning by gaining all the knowledge possible as the word *game* refers to knowledge, and that's what this book is about.

It's not about using people or taking an advantage of people or even playing people, it's about knowledge—knowledge about how people work so that you may work this life to your best ability. And it is through knowing how people work that you will have the ability to do so. Another thing that will help you to be successful is keeping a positive mind-set. A positive mind-set along with a strong desire to win is just as important as having the skills needed to pull off a win.

## Time

One of the most important things that will lead you to winning in life is making sure that you are spending your time in the right places. It may be helpful to sit down and figure this out by writing up a time sheet. This time sheet should be based off of a twenty-four-hour time frame, figuring out how many hours a day you spend doing whatever it is you're doing. So in twenty-four hours, you should be getting around eight hours of sleep a night which would leave you with sixteen hours. Now if you work a nine-to-five job, then you probably work eight hours on a typical day which leaves you with only eight hours of your time.

However, these eight hours are the exact amount of hours that you work every day. So if you can be productive and successful at work during an eight-hour time period, then there's no reason why you shouldn't be doing things that are productive to the other aspects of your life. If you waste your time doing counterproductive activities, then it will show in your personal time sheet. One of the things that is common for people to do is to think that they can operate at a rate that is much higher than they really can. For an example, I hear people say all the time that they're going to give 110 percent or 130 percent. Well, this makes no sense.

All we can ever give is 100 percent of our time, energy, and our attention to the things that are going on in our lives, so if we give 50 percent of our time, energy, and attention to any one thing, we are only left with 50 percent of our attention left.

A good way to look at this is by turning percent into cents, so if you were to have a hundred cents and you were to give twenty cents away, you will be left with eighty cents. Now you can spend your eighty cents wherever you like, but if you spend it all in one place, then you won't have any more time and attention to give elsewhere as everything you do will require your time and energy along with your thoughts and attention.

So by converting percents into cents, you can see that we are limited on how much we are capable of taking on as your time is precious, and we are only allotted so much time, so we must not allow people that aren't worth our time to be taking our time. As sometimes, the things that we're not doing are just as important as the things we are doing. It may also be helpful to write up a not-to-do list as so many people write to-do lists so that they may keep track of the things they need to do, forgetting about the things that they don't want to be doing because they are counterproductive.

Another thing that is common in people is the fact that there are so many different possibilities of different things that one can be doing with their time to the point they become overwhelmed and don't end up doing anything.

So you must zero in on whatever it is you want to spend your time doing. If you aren't sure, I suggest that you simply sit down and seriously ask yourself.

Set boundaries for the people in your life but set boundaries for yourself as well, as this will help you to keep steady.

As the person that has no boundaries may be free to do whatever they want, however, there are far too many possibilities when you have no boundaries for yourself to the point that you become overwhelmed and end up doing nothing.

When the person that sets boundaries for themselves will be more productive because it allows you to actually have more true possibilities for yourself, as you will find that one is actually able to be freer to do whatever it is you want within the boundaries that you set for yourself than those that have no boundaries simply because it narrows down the possibilities that seem possible when they might not even be possible in the first place. As it seems, the mind-set of *anything is possible* is only helpful when operating within these boundaries. This is because when there is too many possibilities, the reality of it is that there really is no possibilities as a person becomes too spread out in their thinking.

These strategies have been developed for you so that you can keep your life on track as game is all about bettering yourself and your life so that you can win in the biggest game of all the game of life.

## Let In or Shut Out

When you're in the presence of another person or let's say multiple people, every move and every action will be one that lets people or shuts people out. When you're really talkative and cheery, of course, people will see this as an invitation of sorts. What it's really doing is letting people know who you are as there is so many different types of personalities. Some people are more serious and more closed off while others may be more outgoing. And of course, if you're closed off, you will be harder to talk to, or another person may be harder to talk to.

However, it is your choice whether you choose to let people in or shut them out. The more you shut someone out, the more they want in, and it is a good strategy to shut people out in the effort to draw them to you, especially the person that would obviously be getting a lot of attention, and that would typically have many people trying to get with them on another level other than being a friend or business partner or anything like that. By shutting these people out, you look different than everybody else as typically others are so quick to let them in as they may be really attractive to others, so they have people that are drawn to them.

When they start to feel as you're not drawn to them, like so many others, they will start to be drawn to you as the mystery of why you're not attracted to them like so many others are will start to eat at them as they start to look for ways to get you to show them some time or attention. So although this may seem like a backward strategy, it's really helpful when dealing with someone that gets a lot of attention. Just remember, every move you make will be showing someone else just who you are, and if you're willing to let them in easily or if you are going to make them work for your time and attention, the truth of it is your goal should always be to get the people around you on your team. The only difference is what strategy you will be using to do so.

## Choose Your Use

As everybody uses everybody for something in one way or another, it will be up to you to choose your use, and although you may think that you don't want to be used for anything, there are many good things that you can be used for. For an example, you can be used for sex, and if you're a male, that can be a good thing. You can be used for a good time because you make someone happy. You can be used for being a solid person or real in your actions. Maybe you can be used for a lot of things, but you want the things that you are being used for to be things that are actually beneficial to you, yourself.

## Subliminal

Subliminal messages are a great way to convey a message to someone without having to be rude or direct as subliminal messages are very indirect and are used to get a point across to someone. They work like this: one may be telling a story to another person right in front of you. If you listen close, they may actually be talking about you, and if you're not paying attention, it might just fly right over your head. Or one may be laughing out loudly about something that feels like the thing they're laughing at is you.

Now although at times people do this to poke fun and to speak to another right in front of your face, but actually behind your back at the same time, these subliminal messages are meant to get you to feel a certain way. And the way they make you feel is inadequate and lesser than. This is a strategy that works as people are always drawn to the people that they are intimidated by. Subliminal messages are also used to let a person know how you feel without ever having to tell them as you must feel as if this other person would catch a clue as subliminal messages are used to convey that it's time for you to leave or that your time is up. Maybe that they really aren't feeling you as subliminal messages are never used to convey happy or good feelings.

## Trickery

Tricking is anytime you give somebody money or possessions in an attempt to gain status, friendship, or sex from someone else. This is a strategy used by people that have no game, as the overall goal is to gain the mind and body of another person since they have no game. They trick their belongings off in the effort to gain what it is they want from you. This is a backward strategy and will be the very thing that we won't be doing, as a person that has game knows there is another way that you can provide one with their needs so that they can draw what they want out of another person.

As anytime you give somebody something without ever getting anything in return, you are tricking. The word tricking off is basically like saying you're fucking off your belongings. When you give people things in the effort to gain the heart and mind, you're unintentionally choosing your use. As you're basically saying, "I'm that person that you can take from without having to give something back in return." The person that has game is looking for this person that is ready to trick off their belongings so that you may advance off of their gameless ways and foolishness.

## In the End

In the end, what it comes down to is your success in life, and you must realize that nobody is going to care about you as much as you care about you. And nobody is going to ever love you more than you love you, and you must realize this so you must stop allowing others to get the best of you, and step your game up to the next level, a level where there is no coming back from. We must stop concerning ourselves with these distractions as that's all people are sometimes, unless we turn these distractions into stepping stones.

Having game is about having this air about yourself that you carry with yourself. This air is filled with confidence and knowing what you want and what you don't want. This air also consists of knowing what other people want so that you aren't taken advantage of at any point. When you have game, you will have options, and having options is what you need to create so that you can open up the ability to make choices.

And it is when you're able to make choices that you can start being the leader of your own and other people's lives. As you know, everyone out here is looking to gain something from you, and the fact that you are aware of that puts you in the position to gain off of them which puts you ahead of the game, as many people are operating out here with no knowledge of how people work. Or the fact that every interaction they have with someone can be a sick game, and you don't want to be the one to lose.

Another part of having game is just stepping your skills up as a person, as your goal should be to be the best you possible. Doesn't matter what you do, you want to be the best at it. And this is why game is so powerful because you can be the best at your job and make great progress only to be taken advantage of by someone that is up on their game.

The fact of the matter is that you need to be a winner in every way. Winning over people is how you're going to accomplish this as you must always look out for yourself over everything, and if you need to take an advantage of others to do so, then so be it because everyone is out for themselves at the end of the day. This is exactly why I make all the suggestions that I have in this book about building yourself up as a person, not only so that you can be looking to better yourself but so that you may do it through stepping your game up.

You want every move you make to be a good move that is beneficial to your life as so many people make bad moves on a daily. They do this by looking for that instant gratification. People that make moves based upon instant gratification are running their game real low on the reward system as the reward they receive will never be that great as some of the greatest rewards will come with long-term sacrifices and relationships.

As there are so many ways to get it out here and if you find yourself not getting money and all the things you desire, then you're going about it all wrong, as everything you do should be accomplished with ease when you go about it in the right way. One of the most desired thing out here is money, and for you to get it, you're going to need to have the skills and knowledge to pull it from the hands of other people in one way or another. Of course, this is going to have to be a legal way. As we have learned, there are no shortcuts in nature. And therefore, there are no shortcuts in life either, and really we are all on a time restriction. So we must use our time wisely, doing the things necessary to advance us in our lives.

So you want to look to organize the people in a winning manner along with knowing what is most important to one's self. By doing so, you may start to get or keep your priorities in order and make sure that you always put the most important things first. One of the most important of your priorities is yourself and your well-being. Although money is up there on the list of priorities, it is my opinion that you should never put money ahead of yourself and your own well-being.

Wherever you are at in life, you should be flourishing in every way, getting bigger, stronger, and adding to your skill set, taking an advantage of all life has to offer, and one of the ways you can do this is by opening up options for yourself so that you can start making choices based on what will help you to be successful and limiting your needs, at the same time, as the person that doesn't have many needs doesn't need much because they already have it or they can get it.

It is my opinion that game originated from women as men always want to have sex with a sexy woman. These women would do anything they could to dress up and to look sexy for these men, not so they could have sex with them, but so they could use the man's desires against him so the women could get what she wanted from the man. This is exactly how the game works. You want to provide the desired needs for someone that is found within you and who you are so that you can get what it is you want from them. Basically, you're just providing people with their needs so you can get your needs met, and this is why you want to cut your needs down by creating options so that you won't need that much from anyone.

In a book I recently read called *Influencing Human Behavior* by Harry A. Overstreet, he says action springs from what we fundamentally desire. This is true as a person is always ready to do what they have to in order to get what they want. This is where game comes into play as you have to make another person want you, and this is what makes them do the things that you want them to as it is through providing a person with their wants that will get them to do what it is that you want them to do. Sometimes all it takes is for you to arouse or bring to the surface a person's wants and needs says Harry A. Overstreet in his book *Influencing Human Behavior*. This is also true as sometimes you may have to remind a person of what they're lacking in their lives by being the person that is able to provide this for them.

The thing that you really don't want to get caught up on is providing people with the things that they need rather than the things that they want, as most people already have the things that they need. It is the things they want that they are typically lacking except for the person that has been lacking the things that they need for so long to the point that the things they want are the things that they need. So when you allow yourself to get caught up on providing the things that you feel they need, you'll find yourself in trouble as you are actually drawing your own self into liking this person more simply by thinking about them too much.

Another reason you don't want to get caught up on providing them strictly with their needs is because you will start thinking of them more than yourself, and it has been proven time after time whenever you concern yourself with someone else's needs over your own, you will be putting yourself on the back burner willingly. Besides, when you become so concerned with someone else's needs over their wants, you may just find that the only thing they really need is for you to leave them alone because it shows that you are clingy and way too interested in providing for them.

This is exactly why you want to provide them with their wants and be the person that they want so that you yourself are the very thing that they want. Then by taking yourself out of the equation or simply stepping back, you may make yourself the very thing that they need. They will need you and want you now simply because they don't have you. They will now want you because you have their needs met within you, just being who you are. You need to talk in terms that another person will understand, and this term that they will understand is their wants and needs.

To understand what another person wants, you will need to be able to see the situation as they do from their perspective and from their current situation they may be in at this very moment. Another way to figure out what a person wants is to understand what they don't want, as the thing that they do want will be the opposite.

Much like fishing, when a person goes fishing for fish, they look to use the correct bait that the fish desire so that they can catch the fish. Now if one was to go fishing with an off-brand type of bait, they might get a few nibbles, but chances are they're not going to catch anything.

However, it is the fisherman that uses the correct bait that is desired by the fish that will bring in the most fish. This is much like with people and when fishing for people, you want to have the correct bait to draw them in.

This is where game comes into play because people desire many different things, and when their desires are fulfilled, they are replaced with new ones. So their wants and needs are forever changing, and so you will need to be ready to constantly change your bait. This is of course unless you want to keep trying to catch the same kind of fish. And by same kind of fish, I mean, people that are needy and thirsty. The bait that you are going fishing with will be your overall look, a combination of your mental, physical, and of course, your verbal game along with all your physical belongings and your qualities and traits that you have to offer another person as it will be these things that you will use for bait in the effort to draw in the fish. Like always, this is of course only so that you may gain all the things that they have to offer.

As there are many times that a woman may sleep with a man just because the man wants to sleep with her, this is because the woman feels that if she gives the man what he wants, then she will get what she wants from the man. Although there are many thirsty men out there that are willing to do anything just to get close to the woman, you don't want to be like them, as it is my opinion that you should work in the same manner. Only sleep with the woman so that you can win her over so that you may gain all the things she has to offer.

There will be many things that you will need to be aware of so that you can be on the defensive side when it comes to having game because in order for you to be successful at running game, you will need to know what things to look for so that you won't get gamed in and taken for a ride. As there are many traits that you will need to be able to recognize from the jump, this is typically referred to as *game recognize game*, and this means that you should be able to recognize game when you see it. However, I have included a list of things to look for on the next page just to refresh your memory and to keep you on your toes.

## To Look For

- Do they spend money on you, or are you always spending money on them? As it must seem obvious that the person that doesn't spend any money on you is only out for their own advancement.
- Lack of spending time as it is where a person spends their time that will determine their interests, so if they don't spend any time on you, then they're not truly interested.
- Lack of trust. When someone doesn't trust you, it is typically because they aren't trustworthy themselves as people tend to see everyone else in the world to be just as they are. This is also because they are aware of the deceitfulness that people are capable of because they are deceitful themselves.
- Control. People that truly like you and care for you will look to give you control over the activities that you may be doing and even control over the things that they will be doing. This is because they want you to be happy and people that get to do what they want are happy as they are getting what they want. People that look to control you are doing so because they have their own agenda, and they care less about you and what you want to be doing.
- Do they try to break you down as a person? As this is a strategy of someone that is running game on you. This is done strictly in the effort to gain control over you.
- Do they have a job? This is very important because if they do not have a job, they must be getting money somehow. And you may just find yourself being their income before you know it.

There may be many, many things to look for in a person to be able to tell if they're playing games or looking to take an advantage of you. However, I only listed a few because after a while it may seem as if everyone is trying to get over on you. This is exactly why I have only included a few of the more typical things to look for in a person so that you will not start to get too overly paranoid about others and the things that stick out as red flags or signs of users.

## Tearing Down

People may try to break you down in many ways so that they can gain control over you. One of the ways this is done is by giving you compliments and making you feel special at first. This is done so that they may build you up before they tear you down. They may even try to lace you with some game pointing out strategies and technics that others may try on you so that you will feel as if they are looking out for you, as if they care when their real intentions are to simply build you up before they break you down.

Now that they have drawn you in and built you up, it is now time to start tearing you down by making you feel stupid in front of other people and criticizing you for the things you do. They will try to allow you to isolate yourself from others and get you all messed up in the head wondering about what they are doing or where they are as they attempt to draw you out of your comfort zone and see just how far you are willing to go. Oftentimes, you may be left feeling confused and as if you can do no right.

It is almost a test to see just how far that you will let them push you as it is when you can push someone so far out of their comfort zone that they'll start to do things that they typically wouldn't do.

And they will start to allow things to go on that they wouldn't typically allow. This is exactly how feelings are formed by making people emotional, as feelings are created through emotions. It is these feelings that are created within you that will be used to break you down. What people are looking to tear down is your sense of self-worth from you. A lot of time, self-worth is taken through shame, so another person will attempt to get you to feel ashamed of yourself. And one of the ways to do this is to cause a chain of events then blame you for them.

When they can actually get you to believe that you are at fault for the problems at hand, they will typically be real unforgiving as it is this shame that they are banking on, using to tear down your self-worth. Another thing they will do is create a problem and watch you scramble to fix it as this shows how attached to them you have become and further shows how far you're willing to go to make things right. As they watch you scramble and attempt to make things right, you may find yourself getting belittled and feeling as if your time doesn't matter, which brings down your sense of self-worth. Meanwhile, you will be building up their sense of self-worth and the value of worth that you may place on them which is actually only drawing you in more and more.

You may even begin to tear yourself down by thinking to or into it and believing the lies that have been put forth. The person that looks to tear you down mentally will also be the person that will tear you down physically, taking items and money from you just as they will with feelings of self-worth and happiness. The whole goal in tearing you down, believe it or not, is to draw you in as your feelings of self-worth diminish. You will find yourself looking up to this person more and more because as your self-worth drops, you will see their self-worth as being worth more than your own.

It is best that you make sure that you do not let anything that another person does to wrong you, just slide.

As the other person will always act as if these events never happened, it will also cause people to view you and your value at a lower level as you're just showing them that it's okay to treat you in such a manner. It is also a typical move of someone that is playing games to try and to confuse you when talking about something they may have done, as this gives them away to not acknowledge guilt or feelings of shame that may come with their actions.

Another trait of the player is to be paranoid about things that aren't typical things that anyone would normally be doing—paranoid about another person cheating, paranoid about the way they feel that others may view them on the account that they know how others must view you being their partner and all.

There is no point in ever trying to prove to someone else that you love them or that you are loyal to them because they already know. If another person was to really think that you are such a terrible person, then they wouldn't want anything to do with you. The fact of the matter is that the accusations are just a way to start or to win a fight. Maybe it's part of their strategy to beat you down as a person, but I assure you, this other person is aware of your qualities, and they know who you really are, so there is no reason to try and to prove it to them.

Your typical player will not love you but love what you can do for them. Love is seen as a weakness. As the saying goes, "Don't be a sucker for love." Players will use the word *love* early on in the relationship in the effort to get you to say it back. This strategy is easy to spot as it is typically said too early on in the relationship for the average person to even have these types of feelings, as players play on feelings, and it is their job to look to create feelings inside of you.

Whether you are the player or the played will be based upon how you play your cards, and as a player, you can always use the fact that someone loves you against them by playing on the feelings that one may have for you will give you an upper hand.

There is a saying that goes like this: "You can't play a player." Well, this obviously isn't true because players play off of feeling, so you can always play a player. As everyone has feelings, it will be up to you to create these feelings using some of the strategies in the book as it is common for players to fall victim to their own game, as it is typically the same thing that builds us up that will tear us down. Meaning, that our strengths are also our weaknesses as well.

The player will never argue with another person unless they do have some feelings toward another person, so basically if a person is willing to argue with you, then they have some feelings of care within them which means that you can play them. The person that doesn't care about you will be the hardest person to play, and this is why we look to create feelings within another person. We create feelings so that we can play off of them which actually just creates more deep feelings within another person to an extent.

This is exactly why you must always keep your guard up because, as we know, everyone is looking to gain in some way or another off of the relationship they have with you. You don't want to put yourself in the position to be played on by another player, as the game goes on and there is no real way to avoid playing these games, unless you plan on being alone your whole life.

There is no sitting out in the game of life. There is no bench for you to sit on like in a game of baseball. It's everywhere you look—at your job at the grocery store, everywhere you go. Your physical, mental, and verbal game will have a value, and it will be assessed by others. Our game will help us in the games we play in the effort to gain the things that we want. As in all games, there is no guarantee that you will win, which means that by playing them you are taking a gamble.

However, it is through the art of game that you may shorten the odds. As this should be your goal anytime, you take a gamble to shorten the odds against you, as there will always be some sort of investment that you will be paying up so that you can be a player in this game that you're playing whether your investing time, love, money, or other belongings. Of course, these games are played in the hopes of advancement. This is where game comes into play because people tend to invest the very thing they expect to get back in their efforts of playing these games. When you have game, you must realize that you don't want to invest the very thing you're hoping to gain out of playing these games.

You want to invest the very thing that is desired by another person so that you can gain what it is that you desire to gain out of this game.

It is the person that invests the very thing that they desire to get back from the game that has no game. As you must look to invest the very thing that someone else desires so that the other party is willing to play, as the games that you choose to play will be up to you, however, it is my opinion that if the games you are playing don't work out to your benefit, then you should either restrategize or choose another game to play.

A game that you are good at, may be the game of love, isn't working for you then it is my opinion that you should change the game that you are choosing to play, not as a cop-out but just a change so that you may continue to advance in another way. However, you want to always focus on the strengths that you have and not so much the weaknesses as the people that you will look to gain from are going to be strong people, and they are not going to make things easy for you, as all people have strengths and weaknesses. And your goal is to get to where you can play with the best of them as it is the strategy of the weak to play on the strengths of other weak people for lack of their own. This means that you need to stay playing the games. We play against good players that have lots to offer. Much like playing a board game, you will not gain anything or very little out of playing against an easy opponent, as all these games we play are just offspring of the bigger game—the game of life. As the saying goes, "Life games reflect life aims," so the games that you play will reflect your direction or goal in life. When these games are played right, meaning for your benefit, they should work together in harmony creating what is called power plays. These power plays are basically large steps or big moves that put you in the position that you want to be in.

These are typically called power moves, and power moves are moves that advance you through life with rapid speed, stepping your game up with the smallest of moves, but they are in the direction that will cause you to advance quickly, shutting down the competition with force showing how strong you really are as you advance with greatness. There is a saying for the Washington State Lottery, and that saying is *you can't win if you don't play*. This is definitely true in all games but especially the game of life, as you must be a strong player if you want to win in life.

The thing that makes life such a game is the fact that, as in all games, there are winners, and there are losers. It is up to you to sharpen your skills and to step your game up in a fashion that is going to propel you to the winning position as life offers so much if you are willing to be the one to take it.

Sex and love are two cards that people love to play off of time. After the time, you will see people attempting to use these to their advantage in the game that they play, as most people would think that sex and love aren't things that should be played off of but feelings that should be felt although these same people do this as well although they will deny it or they don't recognize it. However, they do it to just as anyone else would at their job in their home life and on the street.

The difference is the person that recognizes they do this will be the person that is up on their game and knows that these two cards are good cards to play, as these two are desired by other people so much that some people bank off of strictly playing these two cards to their advantage. However, it is my opinion that there are many other things that people desire out of life. And so there are many other plays to be made, and it is the people that only play on these two cards aren't playing with a full deck.

When people look to play the love card, what they are looking to gain is trust. This is because trust is power, and when you trust someone, you give them power over you. Trust is something that is gained with time, so it must be an obvious sign of someone that cannot be trusted—to look to gain your trust as there will always be an ulterior motive for a person that looks to gain your trust.

## Trust

When you trust someone, it gives them power over you as they will now have the power to hurt you. They will have the power to take from you as your newly found trust comes with certain responsibilities. When you trust someone, you will be giving them power over you and your belongings. This is exactly why people that say the words *you can trust me* aren't trustworthy as they will have another reason why they want you to trust them. And that is so they can take an advantage of you and your belongings that are put forth when you trust someone.

As typically trust comes with time and is something that is earned not given, so you need to be careful who you choose to trust, and this means that you need to be aware of this when you decide what role another will play in your life. This is not to say that you should never trust anyone. This is just saying that it is very important who you choose to trust and realize just what you're giving away when you choose to trust somebody. You're giving up power over you, and who wants to do that? So do not give your trust or power away so quickly.

As there are no moral victories when we're talking about the games that people play in the effort for their advancement, it is very typical for people to say the words "What, you don't trust me?"

Trust is power, and you must know that people will be willing to say anything that they need to so that they can gain this trust. You must know that anytime someone is trying to gain your trust is what they're trying to do or ask for is power over you. Like I explained earlier, there are no moral victories to be gained out here. Believe me, you don't want to be the person that is losing all their belongings and self-respect and is left out here with nothing, still thinking that they're a better person morally because, like I explained, there are no moral victories to be gained. To avoid being sucked in by those that want to grill you over, whether you trust them or not, is to just say no. "No, I don't trust you or anybody."

To trust someone is a lot like loving someone as nobody in this world can hurt you unless you allow them to. Just like trusting somebody is giving them power over you, loving them gives them power over you, your belongings and gives someone the power to hurt you. Of course, these are two things, trust and love, that a player is looking to gain so that they can take advantage of you, and this is why you must be up on your game so that you are on your toes, and you don't make the mistake of giving the wrong person any type of power over you. So you may have to love from a distance, but it's for your own benefit to do so as it keeps you from being hurt and taken for a ride.

## Follow the Evidence

There is no need to ever have to question the things that someone is doing because typically they will lie. As it is very common for people to say whatever they have to so that they don't mess up the relationship they may have with you, so if you want to get to the truth, just follow the evidence wherever it takes you, as it is also common for people to question the evidence at hand. With them being no reason to ask questions that you already know the answer to, you should just follow the evidence wherever it may take you.

One of the first things that a person that is ashamed of their actions will say is *I wouldn't do that. Why would I do that? It makes no sense.* And although you may find yourself agreeing that it doesn't make no sense, do not let yourself fall for this, as it might not make no sense, but that doesn't mean that it isn't true. If you always follow the evidence wherever it might take you, here will be the truth. As the old saying goes, "If it walks like a duck and quacks like a duck, it's probably a duck." Although these sayings may seem a little cliché, these sayings have been around for so long because they are so spot-on.

The truth is, people will do what you let them do, and if you allow them to take an advantage of you, they will. So it is up to you to make sure that you are aware of the ways that people are. This is just the way it is. At the end of the day, we are all people with the need to live and the desire to live good and to be great. There are many ways to accomplish these; however, when you have game and are up on your physical game, life will be a lot easier.

Life is easier when you know who you are and why you do the things you do, just as it is easier when you are aware of the wants and needs that other people are looking to fulfill for themselves. This is exactly how you may now get your needs met by simply knowing what they are and how you're going to get them. Much like a business, you must have something to offer to a possible client so you can get them in the door. Although you may have gotten what you wanted when you leave the store, it is the business that achieves their goal of bringing in that money they need for the bills.

It's when you are able to provide others with what they want, you will be able to get what you want from them. However, what happens when you are providing people with what you feel they need and they still do you wrong? Well, the answer to that is that you may not be able to provide what it is they desire at the moment as there are so many different things that people desire; however, you must not ever let someone do you wrong in any manner because if you do, it will be no one's fault but your own for allowing them to do so, as people only do what you allow them to do. If you didn't allow it, then it wouldn't be going on. It is up to you to set boundaries and limitations as well as expectations, letting people know exactly what you expect from them. When one doesn't follow the expectations and wants to be disrespectful, then you will need to show them instead of telling them what you're gonna do about this. As we know, disrespect just leads to more disrespect; besides, nobody really expects another person to go through with their threats until they are believable through action.

It has been seen over and over again how people try to get you to conform to doing whatever it is they want you to do through threats, much like a child would test one's parents to see what their limits are. Grown adults will do this as well, and they do it to test your limits but also to stretch the limits as well. This is why, in my opinion, if you don't want someone to do something, then you simply don't let them because they will do whatever you let them do.

One of the main things that you want to avoid is allowing people to gain any type of control over you, your actions, and your feelings, as this should be your goal—to gain power over another person's feelings so that you may control their actions. And so you must keep them from doing this to you by letting your feelings get out of control and allowing them to grow too much for any one person as you should always love yourself more than anyone. Being predictable is another thing that will allow people to know what your next play will be, and this gives them the opportunity to control you through their own actions.

Another thing that you want to do is to make sure that you don't allow yourself to react in a poor manner to someone's actions as some people allow others to control another's actions because they are aware of how one will react to a specific action.

If you can't control your own reactions, then you won't be able to control your actions, and if you can't do that, then how do you ever expect to control another's actions as a person is not able to control another's actions directly? However, we can control another's actions indirectly through knowing how they will act when we do or say something, and we know what to do in the effort to get the response that we desire.

This is the reason we must keep our feelings under control because this is where our actions come from. When looking to get someone to do something for you, you must make them want to do the deed for you voluntarily or through knowing how they are and knowing just what to say or do to get the correct action out of them. In the book *48 Laws of Power* written by Robert Green, law 8 says, "When you force others to act, you are the one in control."

This is obviously true as when you act first, it makes things be about you and not so much them, as you always want the focus to be on you and your actions making others work around you and your schedule.

Another thing that people will try to do is rush you. Don't ever let anyone rush you as they are on your time, not the other way around.

You want others to be watching your every move as all their thoughts become consumed with what you are doing, as you lead in the correct direction so that others will follow your lead. When you become so worried about what other people are doing, then you can't think about what you're doing, and people are attracted to leaders, someone that isn't afraid to take charge of the situation and their own lives someone that has direction and that isn't afraid to tell people no.

When you let yourself become consumed with what others are doing, what you're doing is allowing them to take charge, as this will mean that you are now following their lead and the direction they are heading in. Since you want to be the one that is in charge and leading the way, then you must not worry about what direction others are heading in. Even if you care for this person in a great deal, you will only push them away by following their lead. Although your feelings will tell you to follow them, if you don't resist this temptation, you will only be pushing them away.

In the book **48 Laws of Power,** law no. 8 continues on to say that it is better to make your opponent come to you abandoning their plans in the process. Which is also true with your opponent being someone that you wish to draw in, you must know if someone is willing to ditch their plans for you. Then they would definitely rather be with you than to be doing anything else as it is at the point that people start to choose doing other things over being with you that you have either hurt this person too many times and let yourself become predictable to others. And they're making this choice because it is in their best interest.

Or they are now more interested in doing other things more than being with you. Either way, you must have lost the heart and mind because when a person is in love with another or is really drawn to them, they lose sight of thinking about themselves and doing things that are in their best interest.

As they say, **blinded by love**, being blinded by love is when a person likes another person so much that they fail to see no wrong in this person as they may allow this person to treat them in ways they never would allow by another, as one may stop seeing things as they really are, and they become caught up on what could be. People that are blinded by love get so caught up in another person they forget about themselves. This is a sure sign of someone that is on your team or blinded by love. When they are willing to drop their plans to be with you, the way that you test this is you tell another that you have other plans.

This will typically make people attempt to make plans of their own as nobody wants to be the undesired and the one left alone while others are out having fun.

A while after you and your plans are already in action, you might want to make a phone call to the other person just to see what they are doing. This also gives the person you are attempting this strategy on a chance to hear the people in the background having fun. This will only make a person want to be around you even more. When doing this, just know that the other person is going to do their best to act as if they're doing the same.

This is the point where you want to ask the person if they want to meet up abandoning their plans. Regardless if they were doing something and had plans or not does not matter, make sure that you are looking to basically take this person on an emotional ride a little bit by not showing up as planned and make sure that you have some silly excuse for not going through with the plans when they call you in the morning, as all these technics are used to draw another person in and at the same time checking the temperature and seeing just what they are willing to go through just to be with you.

Another law in the book *48 Laws of Power* that stood out to me was law no. 3. Law no. 3 says, "Keep people off balanced and in the dark by never revealing your purpose behind your actions." If they have no clue what you're up to, then they can't prepare for a defense. I agree with this as well, as people will be trying to figure out just why you may be doing the things that you're doing as they may not make any sense

Well, that's good because your goal is to draw them into a point that they're too deep to go back. In the process, confusion is good as it keeps people wondering and guessing about you. As the mystery is always greater than the reality of what you're doing and, as we know, all you're really doing is drawing them in, in the coldest way, you always want to seem as if you have the most going on because it draws people in. You may even tell people that you're going out for the night then just going to bed instead. This will draw people in as it makes them happy to get some of your time.

As people will desire your time, if your time is worth a value and the thing that makes your time worth a value is when other people want it or if other people can't get it, so by making your time worth a high value, you are making yourself desired greatly. And what makes your time worth a value is when others have to fight to get your time, which makes you even more desirable when people have to do the most just to get some time and attention.

Just as you want to provide people with their needs so they will be drawn to you, you will need to keep these people dependent on you to provide these needs as well. This means that you will need to eliminate anyone that seems like a threat to you as this will be the person that can also provide these needs for the person you are looking to game in.

When you keep someone dependent on you to provide them with their needs, it causes one to feel as if you may be the perfect person to do so, which will keep them from looking to find a new person to provide these needs no matter what type of games you choose to play. However, make sure that the games you do choose to play are played for a reason, making sure that the games you make others play are worthwhile games, meaning that the end result of the game will be one worth winning and one that is fun to play as people will not play games that aren't worth playing.

As you may need to play a few games in order to accomplish this, remember when playing games that you do not play games that will damage your reputation and discredit who you are as a person, as your image is everything. As your image is how others see you as a person, your goal should be to get one to view you in a positive way. This is because you are attempting to always be drawing people to you. Your reputation or image is everything when we are talking about game because it is how others will view you and is commonly the deciding factor in whether or not they will like you and will be drawn to you or not.

People will often make investments in people hoping to get a good return on their investment and when they feel as if their investment isn't going to pay off. They may get upset with the person they are investing in, and this can be a technic that you may use to your advantage.

As anytime you can create feelings within someone, it doesn't matter if their good or bad feelings are something that you can always play off of. As mental investments are something you don't want to get caught up on trying to make some mental investments of your own, this is because often they will leave you emotionally broke.

Much like an investment of any kind, they are done with the hopes of a good return. Now you want to let others invest their time and emotions into you. Whether they get a return or not, it does not matter. What matters is that they are willing to invest with you. Once you get someone that is willing to invest with you, then you got action. If someone will invest in you emotionally, then they are already invested in you physically. The way you get them to invest in you mentally or emotionally, you will need to be a good listener.

As a sympathetic ear is something that is typically not that easy to find.

Your goal is to make another person feel as if you understand them and that you are sympathetic to their situation. This in itself will cause people to be drawn to you along with a huge deposit in the emotional bank account that is going to be used to your advantage. Remember to never use the things that are talked about or invested within. You are never used against another person because it breaks trust.

The idea is to allow others to invest within you, not the other way around. You get these investments through time and continuous contact with someone as all relationships are built through continuous contact. These investments are made through being there for someone mentally as they spill out all the things that they feel nobody understands them on. Now this doesn't mean that you are the person to listen to on talk about their relationship problems. This means that you are a mental support for all the other problems one may have.

When you are there for someone, mentally and emotionally, it will draw them to you and make them dependent on you. And of course, as in almost all game strategies, you must take this away from one after you have made sure that they need you for this emotional support. This is because when you are able to make someone an emotional wreck without you, then you have just created feelings within them, as these emotions that one may feel when you're not around will draw a strong desire to have you around.

When you're there for someone emotionally, your goal should always be to hear their problem, and then make them either feel good about the problem or to just make them happy for the time being. When you're able to do this, it shows a person that you will be there for them in their time of need.

## Inner and Outer

Inner beauty is key in outer beauty, and it is the beauty that one holds that will attract others to you as it is very common for a person to be surprised when they meet a solid, good-hearted person that is with the shit, as it is common for people to be one way or another as to say they may have game and are with the shit, but they lack any truly good qualities about them. And the same goes for people that have good qualities and traits about them, but they lack any game qualities that come with the harshness that life can bring which makes them weak.

Just as your game will draw people to you, one of the things that will take your game to the next level is adding good qualities and traits to your game as this will draw people to you. To do this, you must start with the inside within who you are as a person. Stepping up the things that you believe in and keeping it real with yourself, as so many people lie to themselves about who they are, how they're viewed by others and make excuses for themselves when there is no reason for this. It makes you an ugly person on the inside which shines through on the outside to where people can see it.

For an example, I ask the question, "Do you believe in God?" Then I ask the question, "Do you believe that you can disrespect God?"

As you may have your own answer for these two questions, your answers should both be the same for both questions.

As some people may say yes to one but not to the other which is the person that would be lying to themselves so they may feel okay with their actions. I ask the question, "Do you think that any one person in the world loves you more than you love you?" Then I ask the question, "Do you love any one person more than you love you?" The answer to both of these questions should be the same.

These questions are set up to get you to start asking yourself questions about yourself. The answers don't matter as much as the simple fact that you are now asking yourself questions about yourself. You are the only one that knows yourself as you do more than anyone else. We just don't have anyone to ask the questions. This exercise is designed to get you in touch with who you really are by asking yourself questions about yourself. You have already begun, keeping it real with yourself if you have answered these questions correctly.

Keeping it real with yourself is the first step to building inner beauty as you must love yourself and appreciate yourself if you want others to love and appreciate you. Having good qualities and thoughts about yourself will shine through for others to see as we must start from the inside building inner beauty for us to ever achieve outer beauty.

A big part of inner beauty is really just being a good-hearted person along with a good personality to match. Some people are really ugly on the inside, meaning they are real evil in their doings, and this can be seen on the outside.

Well, this is why creating inner beauty by being a beautiful person on the inside will shine through. And people will see this, and they will love you for it. Now this would also mean that you are not a sucker as being a fool will never attract people to you for any good reasons

## You Are What You Do

We are what we do. This means that whatever you do can be looked at as a window into who you are. Here are some simple examples. If you do scandalous things, then you'll be scandalous. If you do dumb shit, you'll be a dumb shit.

If you do cool shit, you'll be cool as shit.

If you do bitch shit, you'll be a bitch.

These are just a few examples, but they explain a lot as people think that they can act however they want, and they feel it's okay. Well, you are what you do, so remember that when or if you feel like doing something scandalous.

## Serving Purpose

Running game is about being successful in your relationships in life, not necessarily having successful relationships but being successful at the end of the relationship. Meaning that you have not been losing in the relationship and overall in life. Because that is the overall goal to be winning and living a good successful life. As we are stronger as a group than we are alone and to gain this group, you're going to have some game to draw the people in that you want in your group. The decisions that we make in life should all be based off of the end result. This is because if we make decisions based off of the now, we will always end up disappointed in life.

So the people that we chose to let in our group and our lives must have a reason to be in our lives, and if they don't, then they must be serving their own purpose when the goal is to get people serving your purpose because it is better for the end result. As the end result of letting people in your life without drawing them in purposely is a life really lived alone, and nobody wants to live alone. Even the person that has people all around them all the time can be the most lonely person as they aren't alone, but they are alone in the world.

And just as you may want to step your game up so that you may get the things you want, it will be through providing people with what they want that will step your game up to the next level. As we have been discussing, there are so many ways to do so; however, you must understand that all of these technics are building you up as a person as it is designed within the strategy, as building yourself up is something that will draw people to you in itself.

Making people see potential within you will draw people to you and have them rooting for you in your corner and have the desire to be on your team as everyone wants to be on a winning team. So at the end of the day, game is really all about building yourself up to where you are desirable by others so that you can draw them in and use what they have to offer to your advantage which puts you in the position where you're winning all around in every way because when the game is over and you come to the end of the road, you want to be sure that you're the winner.

Game can be anything that you have that will draw people to you. So if you have a good personality, it will be something that draws people to you. However, you don't ever want to simply have one or two things about yourself that draws people to you because it puts you in the position to be played or used. If you are played or used, make sure it's for something you wouldn't mind giving up.

You want people to build you up not tear you down; however, people that want to tear you down can be used to your advantage as well. As anytime you know what someone else wants, you will be able to find a way to use them to your advantage. However, you want people to be drawn to you like no other, and you will find that if you follow the strategies in this book, it's through building up who you are as a person that people will be drawn to you. Just be aware, just as you are drawn to them for something, they will be drawn to you too for something. And if they're not drawn to you, then you must arouse something within them that is.

Another thing that people are drawn to is drama. Whether you realize it or not, people become addicted to drama and the lifestyle that comes with it. If you are unsuccessful at running game, you can always run drama: running drama is a strategy used by people that are playing games, not running game as there is a difference. For example, people that are playing games tend to lie as it is necessary for them to work their strategies on you. People that are running game do not lie as there is no reason for it.

Lying also breaks trust and will cause people to lie to you as well. Then they find out that you are lying. So for people running game, it is not helpful to their game as game is meant to draw people in, not push them away.

Another difference between people that are running game and those that are playing games is arguing, as people that are playing games will need to argue as it is part of their games that they play. They will argue with you when the time is right so that they can get you to do whatever it is that they want as they may want some money from you, so they'll say things that simply aren't true, something like this: you never give me money, or as soon as you get money, you leave. These words are meant to get you to attempt to prove them wrong and give them some money.

Another reason people playing games like to argue is because they can control whether you are coming or going simply by being nice to you one minute then they may start an argument with you just to get you to leave. This argument typically will make no sense. However, it is the strategy of the person that is playing games. However, the person that is running game will look to eliminate arguments as there is no need for them. Arguments also push people away, and they are a good way to lose the heart and mind. Of course, when running game, the idea is to draw people in, and people that are drawn to you will look to make sure that they are pleasing you in every way.

People that are playing games allow themselves to get lost in the moment that others created in the effort to draw them in. This is because people that play games typically don't have any real, true game. And so they allow others that do have game to create these moments they'll get lost in.

On the other hand, people that have game know that it is up to them to create the moment that another person will get caught up in. Again, this is because it draws people in however the reason for running game, and playing games is the same. They're just different ways of going about getting the things that you desire out of people.

Although I don't recommend playing games, you may have to play some games sometimes in the effort to get people to do what you want them to do. Another difference in people playing games and people running game is people that are playing games will tend to play into their own bs as they get lost playing the games that they created, as they may sometimes become very paranoid thinking that everyone is trying to play them in some kind of way or another. This is typically referred to as lost in the sauce. This is when a person will start to get to the point that they take everything way to serious as they start to be unable to tell the difference between reality and what is just part of their game.

A person that is running game knows better as there is no game that is being played on such a sick intellectual level, only the game that is being run to draw people in and to get what is desired along with knowing how to get it, without ever playing any sick games that one may get lost in their self.

The person that has game and is running game will know better when they hear some bs that is clearly just that—bs. The person that is running game will know not to entertain that bs because it just leads to playing games with one's self.

The person that is playing games will tend to get lost in their own games that they play losing track of their ultimate, overall goal, which is to be always making your life better for yourself. They become caught up on simply making sure that they feel they are the ones running the games that they are playing while the person that is running game on others will not allow people to be in their life, if they are making one's life more difficult. This is because anyone that is making your life worse than it already is will be the person that is no longer thinking about you but themselves as they have simply stopped thinking of what you want, and they are now thinking of themselves.

It is my opinion that if someone makes your life worse, then you don't need them in your life. However, if they make your life better, then it only makes sense that, in my opinion, one does need them in their life. It's pretty simple; however, this is something that many people don't stop to think about whether or not if someone is making their life better or worse.

People that are playing games will tend to get lost in their own arguments and game, playing ways to the point they may sometimes attempt to prove a fact that they already know to be true to another. As they attempt to prove one wrong in an argument, however, the person that is running game knows that there is no need to confirm what they already know to be true. Of course, there is no need to ever argue with anyone because there is no winning an argument, much like there is no need to ever try to prove something to another person.

As it is my opinion, if you know something to be true, then why would you have to get caught up on trying to prove it to another person. The truth is if you do this, you may be just playing into another person's sick game and entertaining their bs. The person that is running game knows the difference between running game and playing games while the person that is simply playing games will tend to not know the difference. As the reason they're playing games in the first place is usually because they have no game or knowledge of game-running strategies.

Game-running strategies are created to build you up in every way. They don't tear you down or take from you in anyway as they are designed to not only build yourself up as a person but to allow or create the atmosphere where the people in your life will be building you up as well.

## Energy

Good energy attracts people like you wouldn't believe, as the energy that you put off will be the energy that you get back. So if you put off a bad energy, then you will most likely get bad energy back. And low energy is what bad energy is mostly comprised of or made of, so in other words, if you have low energy, then you're most likely giving off bad energy, and this will be the same energy or feeling that others will put back onto you. As nobody wants to be around a Debby Downer or somebody that is depressed or unhappy.

Good energy or high energy brings about a heightened sense of awareness and cranks your personality into overdrive and brings out the great personality that you already have. When you have good energy or high energy about yourself, it brings about a happiness within yourself and in others. Good energy or high energy is what sparks creativity from within. This creativity is what arouses your sense of humor in yourself and within others as well. As this creativity will bring about things that usually wouldn't be looked at in such a funny manner until it is seen through the point of view that you present. This point of view would never be brought about if it wasn't for this high or good energy.

This high or good energy is contagious and will always work in your favor to draw people to you, as people will always be drawn to good or high-energy type of people.

In a book called *7 Habits of Highly Effective People*, it talks about an energy that is created when two energies come together. This energy is called synergy, and synergy is what causes creativity to flow as two energies are combined. This creativity is what brings about new possibilities as the creativity flows through the air like water flowing down a river, peacefully and gracefully flowing, never knowing where this water may take you as the possibilities are endless.

As we know, new possibilities are sparked and brought about through new perspective. As new perspective is one of the five keys to game, as anytime you can provide new perspective for someone, you may bring about new possibilities, and new possibilities is the very thing that most people are missing in their lives. This is why people are drawn to the people that can provide these new possibilities for them, as there aren't that many people that view life in a manner that can change the way another person views them.

All these things are brought about through energy and not just any energy but high energy or good energy as these two can be viewed as one in the same. So simply by ramping up your energy levels, you may be able to draw people to you in a good fashion as good energy brings good energy, ramps up your personality, parks creativity, and brings about new perspective.

## Act

If a person can act a certain way, dress a certain way, and be a certain way even if just for a short time, then for that time, no matter how long they are able to pull it off for, they actually are another person in a way, much like an actor or an actress that is able to change their clothes and their personality for the scene that they are in. You can do this too as you are in control of your body, the clothes you wear, and how you act, much like a movie star would. You can change who you are on your outside appearance through changing your clothes, your typical moods or actions, and even who you are.

For an example, everybody has a specific way that they act when they go to court. They are typically really respectful of the judge and will typically wear nice clothes and act as if they're innocent. When really, they're anything but innocent, just as people that go to their job and they tend to act another way when they're at their job as well. However, when they get home, they are free to act however they want to. So I ask the question, "Does this make you fake? Or does this simply mean that you act the way you are required to do so that you can get the desired outcome that you want?" If you ask me, there are many times that we, as people, are required to act a specific way in order to get what we want.

And it's only frowned upon by people that are not able to harness this ability and to use it against others in the effort to get what we want. This isn't nearly as bad as it sounds because, again, to get what you want, you will have to give others what they want. So if you have to change who you are for a moment to play the role of the person, that is desired by another person, just so that you can get what you want through becoming who you need to be to get it.

So you may alter everything about yourself, if need be for a moment, in order to get what you want. And at times, you may be required to do so which may raise the question, "Why not just continue to be this character that you are playing?"

And the truth of the matter is that you can continue to play the role of being anyone that you want for as long as you want. However, you will need to alter your character from time to time to fit the desire of others. However, you are who you are, and I wouldn't ever say that's right or wrong, keeping in mind that you want to be the best you that you possibly can be.

This simply means that you want to be that light that lights up the room when you walk into one, keeping up on your three parts of game, physical, mental, verbal, along with making sure that you are not offensive to others in your presence as this only pushes people away.

This is all part of being who you need to be so that you can get what you want. As we know, everybody wants someone that is going to take them away from the situation that they're in. As everyone wants to be in a better situation than they're currently in even if they're rich, everybody wants to step their life and their situation up into an even better place.

As it seems, people are always wanting more, and they want to keep building on the lives that we already have. This is why you will always be able to offer another person something that is either better than what they currently have or simply something new, as everybody always wants something new and fresh, a change from what they are used to. And people simply get bored with the things that they do have, and they become complacent. This would be the perfect time for you to run game, providing another with something that they never knew they were needing.

## Keep Your Head in the Game

You always want to keep your head in the game, meaning that you are always aware of the position that you hold that others in your life are holding along with your goal and keeping aware of what others around you are attempting to do. Or the reason that they are in your life is everyone in your life will have their own purpose.

Keeping your head in the game is about awareness, and keeping your goals is the main focus, never forgetting how the game goes.

The game will always be in favor of those that play it right, and of course, playing the game right is about being the successor in the game, as there are many times that we may lose track of our goals, getting caught up on the small things that have little to no value.

One of the main things that we get caught up on is looking like the man stunting on people that don't have the skills to pay the bills, so to speak. This only drags us down, creating a group of people that are wanting to take your success from you. Putting people up on the game is also dangerous as it can sometimes end up not in your favor or best interest. As putting people up on game is to say that you're putting them up on valuable information, as knowledge is power, and to have this knowledge means that you have power, and handing someone power is typically not a good idea unless you intend to use it against them at the end of the day.

Although keeping your head in the game is more about not forgetting what you came for and not letting others intrude on your advancements that you are looking to gain as a person, when you stop keeping your head in the game, you will see that others will take advantage of you in the same moment that you are caught slipping and starting to allow your thoughts to run wild and not keeping them in the game.

## Pin 'Em Against Each Other

Any chance you get to pin one person against another can be looked at as a good opportunity, as this only draws both parties toward you as they both attempt to gain you and your support. When you have two or more people interested in you, pinning them against each other will only draw them closer to you as they become in competition with one another, as both people will become aware that you have options and that you don't need to settle for less. It also lets people know that you are wanted which also draws them to you as well, as both parties will look to attempt to please you on every and any level possible to the point that it becomes a fight to win you over at all costs, putting you up on a pedestal as if you are someone so special that there is a reason to fight over you. In fact, others on the outside looking in will actually be drawn to you as well, just witnessing how others are willing to fight over you. This makes others feel there must be a good reason to be fighting over you. Another reason that you want to pin people against each other is because it puts you in the position where you can do no wrong. As both people are fighting to please you, they never suspect that it's been your strategy all along to pin one against another.

In fact, this strategy works so well because it is the last thing that you will ever want for these two people to become friends. If they become friends, you will find yourself being the one that is left in the dust as neither one will want anything to do with you, as this will take all the mystery out of the relationship and cause the two people that you would have pinned against each other to gang up on you. They may start to team up pointing out your flaws and other reasons why not to like you. This is why you always want to use this strategy to your advantage before others will find a way to use the fact that you failed to pin one against another when you had the chance to. This strategy is used time and time again and is easy to point out, if you know what to look for. People that are looking to pin you against another person will typically do so by telling you a lie about the other person then they tell the other person a lie against **you** in an attempt to pin you against the other person. The best way to pin a person against another person is through jealousy, as it is through jealousy that you may create the atmosphere for these two people to pin themselves against the other person. You just simply create the atmosphere for the two of them to do so through picking and choosing which one you will give your time to today. You will make the other one jealous and allow them to pin themselves against each other.

## Contest for Amusement

If you look up the word **game** in the English dictionary, you will see that the definition says a contest for amusement. Now for a lot of people, that's exactly what they run game for—their amusement, as they are entertained by the things people are willing to do for them when running game or playing games. However, it is my opinion that it is lame to run games or play games for amusement. Although it is easy to become drawn to things that amuse you, do not lose track of your goal and keep your head in the game as it is equally lame to be okay with being someone else's entertainment.

As this is no contest for amusement, this is your life, and your goal is to get results out of running game.

These results should be the very thing that gets you to the place in your life where you're living good. As for the contest, there is none, as the strategies in this book are designed to draw people to you while building up who you are at the same time, putting you in a position where there is no contest for you as the only others that you would have to contend with would be players or people that are on your level which there are none. The only contest is for others to contend with each other to attempt to gain your heart and mind along with all that you have to offer.

This is why game is so powerful because it puts you in the position where others will attempt to gain your heart and mind. When gaining the heart and mind becomes nearly impossible, as the things that you have learned will give you a new mind-set, that comes with new thoughts that will set both your heart and mind in the proper place, and that is on yourself and for your own advancement.

You may learn some good strategies and technics in this book; however, the main thing that you will retain from reading this book is a whole new mind-set that will get you back into focus on the real goals that we may have forgotten about. This absentmindedness comes from the game strategies and technics that are described in this book. Whether you choose to harness them or become a victim to them is up to you. However, it is the awareness of these games that will give you an edge over others, although there have been a variety of different topics talked about through this book. This is because game is knowledge and whatever knowledge you can add to your game can be used in a beneficial manner, as the more knowledge you have, the better you can use it for your advantage.

## Motivation

It is very important for you to understand what motivates people so that you may gain control over any situation, as you always want to make you yourself become the very thing that will motivate others to do the things they do.

This is so that you may have control over their actions as you become the driving force that gets people motivated to eventually be working toward your goals just as you do. Everybody has different things that will motivate them, so what will motivate a person will be different for each person.

Some people are money motivated while others are sex motivated or even friend or family motivated. You must figure out what motivates people so that you yourself can use this motivation against another in the effort to get them to do what you want them to do. It is my opinion that the best thing to be motivated by is goals. If you yourself are motivated by accomplishing goals, it will help you to stay focused and will draw people to you as well when they see that you are accomplishing goals, as this makes you look as if you have a direction, and people are drawn to others that have direction.

However, it's always best to keep the exact nature of your goals a secret because when others know exactly what goals you intend on achieving, they will know exactly what motivates you, and then they will be able to play you to their advantage. This is because when you know what motivates a person, you will also know what will control a person. So to keep control over the situation, you must never let another know just what motivates you. So you want to keep some mystery in the situation to an extent so that you may almost keep people guessing.

People fear the unknown, and fear is another thing that motivates people as well. If you can make people fear you or fear what it is that they don't quite understand about you, it will motivate people to do things, the things that you want them to do to be exact. Another big-time motivator is love, as people are always so willing to do things for love. So if you don't know what a person is motivated by, fear and love will always motivate another to do whatever you want them to do as well.

You can become another person's motivation when you yourself make someone want to be a better person as well, as everybody wants to be a better person, and when you make another person feel this way, then you yourself will in fact become their motivation. If this person doesn't recognize this, you can always help them to recognize this by simply taking yourself temporarily out of the occasion.

## Many Interests

When it comes to people that are in multiple relationships and have multiple love interests, it is my opinion that it's much better to be the side boyfriend or side dude; however, you want to say that it doesn't matter. These two mean the same thing. The reason I say this is because the side guy is there to have fun, make money, and to have lots of good sex while the main boyfriend is the guy that gets cheated on and goes through the tough times and pays all the bills.

When it comes to women, all women want to be the main girlfriend, and they will fight over this position.

As women are drawn to men that other women like, the side girlfriend or side girl is only present to fulfill the needs that one may desire when they're not being fulfilled by the main girlfriend. This is why it's important to make yourself the perfect provider for another because they will search to get their needs met somewhere else, if they're not being met at home, and this is why you want to be aware of another's needs and provide them.

One of the main things that will allow another to have a side girlfriend or side boyfriend is time. When you give another person the time to find another, they can, and they will if their needs aren't being met. So when you notice that another is having large amounts of time that are not accounted for, then you must be aware that you are giving them the space and the time along with a reason, if you're not satisfying their needs. It's just a fact of life that people have needs, and as people, we will find a way to get those needs met. In fact, it can almost be a test to see if you are fulfilling someone's needs by simply giving them some alone time and then watch what they do with it.

When you start having multiple love interests, the goal is to keep them a secret as when they are found out it will cause mass mayhem as this isn't your goal. One of the main reasons men will start to have multiple love interests is because they want to feel as if they're the man, as if they're somebody special, and they are wanted. However, it is very typical for women to develop these same feelings, so the road goes both ways for men and women. So much like how you game another in by providing them with their needs, you will need to continue to provide them with their needs, if you wish to keep them around.

However, you must be aware when you start to have multiple partners, you will find yourself playing games instead of just running game. And you will run the risk of losing the heart and mind of the original partner.

## Shock and Awe

I call this the shock-and-awe technic. This is where you come with an overwhelming whirlwind of new information that will draw people in like a cyclone changing the way they view things, bringing a new perspective and point of view on how we shall approach getting the things that a person will typically need along with the goal of living a good life, as this is typically most people's goal in life.

There are many things required to make this good life possible. You want to appear as if you are aware of what needs to happen to make all this possible along with making yourself appear to be the solution to gaining this good life that everybody so desires. You make yourself the solution by having a solution and incorporating yourself within this solution. However, the way the shock-and-awe strategy works is by coming with all this information like a whirlwind, of course, when the time is right, leaving the person you wish to draw in almost just stunned as they can't believe they have met someone that has the solutions to all their problems. The reason you want to lay it on them in such a quick manner is because it makes you seem true at heart.

Remember, the goal is to overwhelm this person to where they are lost for words. Timing is everything as you do not want to hit them with all this info at the wrong time because it will only push people away. The right time will always present itself and should be obvious to one. However, if it doesn't seem obvious, then just know it will be long after you get their attention and have their interests within you sparked long after you allow the other to spout off about who they are as people love to do this.

People are intimidated by people that seem superior to them which actually will draw people to you. There are many ways you can make yourself appear superior to someone. However, you can start with your first impression as it is the first impression that will be the lasting impression.

With nobody really knowing who you are until you open your mouth, people will judge you on the things that seem obvious from the gate. That would be your body language, how you carry yourself, how you dress, and whether you have a clean-cut image or a shaggy one, as all these things can be seen before you ever say a word to a person. It is my opinion that the less you say, the better; however, confidence goes a long way, and it is this confidence that you carry with you that will give confirmation to another when you do start to speak.

People love to be right, and you will see time after time people will look to find reasons to prove themselves right, and this is why it is so important to give off the best first impression possible, so they will look to prove themselves right on the assumptions they made on you.

## Stability

Stability and success is another thing that people are drawn to as well. So whenever you can provide stability and success, then people will be drawn to you as well. If you can't provide stability and you're not successful, people will still be drawn to you if you can manage to look successful. Just as people will be drawn to you if you show that you can provide stability, whether you can or cannot doesn't really matter so much if you can play the part of someone that can.

To do this, you may have to play some games and, most of all, look the part.

This would mean that you dress nice, and the people around you say good things about you. As we know when running game, your appearance and your reputation are everything. So keeping up a good appearance will also help your reputation as you don't want a poor appearance or reputation. And, of course, when trying to appear successful and you don't have visible success such as money that typically comes with success, you may have to act as if you do have some things going for yourself. However, I ask the question, "If you're going to act as if you're someone else, why not just put in the work to become the person that you want to be?"

# Chapter 9

# So Random

> We must keep our focus the same and our strategies ever changing as opportunities will present themselves in many different ways. We must be willing to adapt to overcome the situation at hand as the world is forever changing. We must not allow this to change our focus.
> —Kelly Buchanan

## Hit and Miss

A HIT-AND-MISS LIST IS A great way to record the areas that you have been successful at as well as the areas that you have not. This hit-and-miss list will be helpful to you in life as well as when running game or even playing games. A hit-and-miss list is exactly that, a list of your successes and your failures. So anytime you attempt to do something, you will find that whatever it is, there will be a place for it somewhere on your hits-and-misses list.

Let's say, for an example, you have set your sights on gaming in someone from your place of work. You may try many different strategies to get their attention, and nothing seems to be working. If you record these hits or misses in your hits-and-misses list, it will help you to see what types of things seemed to spark their interest. This will be helpful in keeping you on track, as not only may you be able to try a new strategy each time but when you look over your hits-and-misses book, a pattern will start to emerge to where you may be able to see very clearly what has been working and what hasn't. This will also be a good sign of what types of topics they're interested in which will also be helpful in letting you know exactly who a person is when you are aware of their likes and interests. It's when you know what a person's likes and interests are that you will be able to provide them, which of course, makes you the very thing that they're interested in.

A hit-and-miss list can be very helpful in many other areas of your life as well. Keeping a running log of what areas you are successful in and what areas you are not, you can use a hit-and-miss list for recording your hits and misses in different areas of investing, as anytime you choose to invest your time your money and your energy, you want to be sure that you're getting a good return, and a hit-and-miss list will help you do so.

## Purpose

It seems that we are all slaves to something, whether it's money, maybe drugs, or sex. The list goes on and on.

So I ask the question, "Are you really in control of your life?" There are many people that feel they have control over their lives when really they have lost all control, as they have become slaves to the things that they feel are almost a requirement for living. When running game, this will definitely be one of your main goals—to get another person to feel as if they need you to live a life worth living.

It is through investing in who you are as a person so that you can become the person that is desired by all. Remember, people live for purpose and meaning, and it is this purpose and meaning that you must provide. One of the ways that you can do this is by maintaining purpose and meaning for yourself in your own life, as people are really drawn to people that have a purpose in life and a strong agenda and overall mission in life. People that recognize this in you will desire to be a part of it due to their own lack of purpose or to the lack of success they have had in reaching their goals or purpose.

There is an old saying, and it goes like this: "If you're going to bet on a horse, then bet on your own horse." This simply saying that there's no better person to bet on than yourself, so if you plan on betting a bet on yourself after all you are capable of putting in the footwork needed to succeed. When really all you need is to be slightly better than the rest to be the best. No one has to be exponentially better than the rest to be the best but just a little bit better than the rest, and that is what makes you the best.

So there's no better person to bet on or invest in than yourself. You can invest in yourself by gaining knowledge and investing the correct qualities and traits required to build the exact person you wish to be. One of the things that will help you with this is a hit-and-miss list as I highly recommend it. One of the things that brings us down as people is something that is commonly seen in athletes. This is what they like to call *peaking*, and peaking is when a person gets to their highest point possible, either in life or on the field, and then they will start to go downhill after they reach their peak.

This is why we must continue to work on who we are forever, never stopping because if we do, then we will slowly start to head downhill. However, if we keep heading one direction through investing within ourselves which includes getting rid of all bad qualities and traits that make up who we are as well, this is because once you acknowledge negative traits within yourself and you do not rid yourself of these negative traits, then you may start to embrace them. This is because once you allow something to be, it's easy to see whatever it is to be acceptable because you are excepting it by allowing it. And when you allow these traits to exist and be acceptable within yourself, it's easy to allow these traits to exist in those around you as well, which means that we must step up the standards we hold on ourselves in order to be able to draw others to have high standards themselves.

This is also a good way to raise the value that you have invested within yourself through investing within who you are as a person as this will make you look like a rich stock or a good investment. As anytime someone is looking to invest in any type of way, they're going to look for the best place to invest. When someone decides to invest themselves and their time in you, that's exactly what they're doing, making an investment with you. This is where the term *emotionally bankrupt* comes from, as a person will invest so heavily with another that when their investments aren't honored, they are left emotionally bankrupt.

This is also why I say, "Do not let yourself get too invested with another person to where you don't feel that you can ever just cut your losses."

On the other hand, when looking to get people to invest in you, you will need to look like a solid investment, one that is sure to come with a good return. So much to the point that your value will shine through for all to recognize, as some people that are already emotionally bankrupt may not have anything left to invest. They may look to hold on to what they have emotionally which would be simply themselves.

This is where having a solid stock or strong qualities that are seen to all comes into play, as you may take it upon yourself to offer some of this priceless stock which would simply be you yourself and your time to another that may be emotionally bankrupt. Just because a person may be emotionally bankrupt doesn't mean that they are financially bankrupt. However, you want to look at it as it is up to you, although it is my opinion that in any case that you remember that you must offer up some kind of services in one way or another to get what you want.

By building yourself up to the point that you are desired highly, you may make yourself the very thing that people want. Once this is done, your time will have a high value to others and can be used to get the things that you desire out of others.

When looking to build up who you are as a person, we do this from the inside out. Working on your character and personality is much like working on a math problem where you may add or subtract different characteristics within your character. Imagine a plain person, a person that has no good or bad character traits about them. At this point, this person has a world of potential, and although they have no good traits that will build this person up, they also don't have any bad traits that will drag one down.

So what kinds of traits would you want to add to this person? Remember that weak-minded traits will only subtract from your character which would only make this person a lesser-than person as there is no room for weak-minded traits unless you're looking to get taken advantage of by the stronger-minded people. There is no limit to the amount of traits and qualities that you can have.

A self-inventory sheet is a great way to inventory the qualities and traits that you currently have. Then if you feel that you would like to get rid of some of these qualities or traits, it is easy to do so by simply not entertaining them, as you can be whoever you want to be.

I ask the question, "If you were walking down the street and you dropped something that you really didn't need, did you really lose something? Or did you simply get rid of some trash that you really didn't need and in the process made some room for other things? This newly found space may leave room for other things that could open up a world of opportunities. As we know, sometimes it's best to simply cut your losses and start a new which is another reason why you want to invest good qualities within yourself, so other people aren't so quick to want to cut their losses with you.

However, for the most part, we know what people want. They want to get the best of us. They want to take all that they can from us money, sex, the sense of self-worth, and so on, and they won't stop looking to advance in any way that they can. The way they are looking to advance is off of us in any and every way that they can. This is why it is so important to stay at the top of our game at all times whether we work on our physical game or who we are on the inside. Everything we do should be in the effort to build ourselves up in every way.

So far, we have covered building ourselves up on the inside and within who we are. We talked about the three parts of game as we have covered many other subjects as well, as all these subjects build us up as people. Having the knowledge to do so is key in succeeding in life. However, one thing we haven't covered is spirituality, as having a strong belief in *God* will help you step your game up as well.

The reason I say this is because it's true, if you were to think about it. Having game is about having this sort of air about yourself that will draw others to you.

This air comes with being the type of person that others desire and are attracted to. Well, this air also comes from being a smart person that knows what's going on out here in the world so that you may use the things that are presented to you in the best of your ability. And God can give you this game or knowledge that can be used to draw others to you.

He can also give you the air of richness that is desired so much by others as this air is what draws them to you. Now whether you believe in God or not is up to you; however, this book is based on facts, and the fact of the matter is that God is definitely real. And that it is through the fear of God that knowledge begins. So I ask the question, "What if you had a perfect world that was somehow created, whether God has created it or if it just simply came to be on its own matter? And let's say some way, somehow, out of nowhere a baby was to somehow appear."

Of course, where this baby came from would be a good question. But let's not focus on that right now. So out of nowhere, a baby was to appear. Who would take care of that baby because as we know babies can't even lift their heads up for the first nine months of their life.

So who would take care of this baby. Surely the baby would be eaten by all the other animals. There would be no mother to feed the baby, and so the baby would simply die. There is no way possible that the baby would survive, and there's no way that we can survive without the blessings of God in our life.

Before you believe in something or someone else, you must first believe in yourself. Once you start to believe in yourself and who you are as a person, then you can start to believe that there is a God and that he has your back. It is my opinion that once you love yourself, then you can start to love and believe in others, even God. However, the reason I'm telling you this is because this book is made up of facts, and the facts are that the word *game* comes from knowledge.

And all knowledge starts with the fear of God. In fact, if it weren't for God being in my life, then I wouldn't be able to put all this knowledge together in this book for you to read now, as I had to love myself before I could ever love any others, and once I started to treat myself well, it became obvious to me that God has always been in my corner waiting for me to step my game up. And it is through my acknowledging this that I have gained that air about myself that naturally draws the things I desire out of life.

## Games

So as I promised in the beginning of the book, we're going to talk about some of the games that people play. One of the most famous games people like to play is the *fake a fight*. The *fake a fight* goes like this: someone will start a fight with you all in the effort to get you to get mad at them, all so they can leave the house or the situation as this gives them a reason to leave and, in some cases, a reason to be gone for days at a time.

Much like the fake-a-fight strategy, people will sometimes be really rude to you, all in the effort to get you to want to leave. This is done so that they can get you to leave instead of them leaving, as nobody wants to be somewhere that they are not wanted, and you can tell when people are using this strategy because they won't have a real reason to even be mad at you. So they will simply be rude to you for absolutely no reason simply so you will leave the place that they are at.

Another game that people like to play is the backward game. This is simply where someone will tell you that you are doing all the wrongful things to them that they are actually doing to you. This is done in the effort to make you mad and to basically start a fight with you.

This is also a good way to get you all messed up in the head to where all you can think about is them. At this point, they will have you all messed up in the head while they are off doing them. However, the main goal in this is to get you angry so they can start a fight with you.

The best way to fight against these games and strategies is to act as if you don't care and that you are aware of what they're doing as well as letting them know that you will do the same. Another thing that will help is if you do not text or call them, as this lets them know that you do care, and your goal is to let them feel as if you're off doing the same things as well. You always want to act as if you are aware of what they're up to and why they're doing what they're doing even if you don't.

Another thing people will always look to do is to confuse you. This is because when you're confused, you will believe anything that they tell you. This strategy is easily recognized because the things they are saying will not make sense. It is when the things they say don't make sense or add up that you will know that they are simply trying to confuse you. As we know, everything happens for a reason. It's the old cause and effect, as nothing in this world happens without cause or a reason for the effect that the cause has caused which is the effect that happens due to the cause. Just remember, there is a reason for everything.

Having game is about having the ability to attract others to you with ease. So the idea is to not try too hard to do this as you should be able to attract others to you without having to really try at all.

However, you will have to change some of the ways that you look at things at first until it starts to come naturally, as people will be drawn to you naturally anyway as everyone is looking to gain something from you.

The idea behind having game is to be able to gain the things that you want from these people. And you do that by simply choosing your use and, of course, making sure that the things they want from you are the things that you want to give as life is really one big game, and so you want to win at the end of the day. You will find it a whole lot easier to get through life when people are drawn to you for the right reasons, reasons that actually benefit you.

If I had to tell you any one thing that you can do to step your game up, it would be to work on your three parts of the game, your physical, mental, and verbal game along with providing new perspective for others, as providing new perspective for another person will draw anyone to you.

Just remember, nobody will ever love you more than you love you so take good care of yourself. Don't ever put anyone else's needs ahead of your own because, at the end of the day, it's you and your life that is the most important.

So keep your head in the game. Keep your focus in the right direction, and above all, love yourself and God because, in the end, that's all you really have.

I hope you have enjoyed the book as it has been an adventure documenting all of these information along with years of hardship, as it took me a long time to figure all of this out; however, I decided that I needed to figure out how all these strategies and technics were played out, and ever since, I've been running game on others. And my life has improved exponentially, and at this point in the game, there's no going back. And really, why would you want to?

## About the Author

My name is Craig Austin Massey. I was born at St. Joseph's Hospital in Tacoma, Washington, in 1984.

Throughout my years living in Tacoma, I have come to realize that it is through the art of game that I have been able to advance in my life. It has taken me years of life experience along with endless studying of human relations and the finding of just how we as people work that I have been able to come up with all the information you read in this book. I decided to write the book because most of the knowledge or game is not shared by those that have harnessed the art. It is typically earned through years of trials and tribulations along with many losses for a person to gain the knowledge that is in this book. As just having game is not enough, if you desire to run game, then you need to know the proper strategies and technics needed to do so. I also felt it was important to write the book so that these strategies and technics can be documented and in clear writing for the person that is getting a game run on them as well because life is hard enough as it is without being part of a game that you are not even aware you're a part of.

I hope you enjoy the book as I know it will help you in your life.

CPSIA information can be obtained
at www.ICGtesting.com
Printed in the USA
BVHW031413180521
607630BV00005B/512